ALLIED SOLDIERS
OF WORLD
WAR TWO

Compiled by Philippe CHARBONNIER
Translated by Jean-Pierre VUILLAUME

Jacques	ALLUCHON		Frédéric	FINEL
Franck	BACHMANN		Jon	GAWNE
Pierre	BESNARD		Gérard	GOROKHOFF
Jean	BOUCHERY		Hervé	HALPHEN
Patrice	BOUCHERY		Jacques	MAIGNON
Eric	CRÉPIN - LEBLOND		Denis	LASSUS
Philippe	CHARBONNIER		Philippe	LAURENT
Robert	D'ÉLIA		Bernard	PETITJEAN
Richard	DE FILIPPI		Jan	RUTKIEWICZ
Michel	DE TREZ		François	VAUVILLIER

ISBN: *2 908 182 27 0*
HISTOIRE ET COLLECTIONS, P.O. Box 327, Poole, Dorset BH 15 2RG UK

CONTENTS

ALLIED SOLDIERS OF WORLD WAR 2

A focus on the most famous and most representative Allied units of World War 2, from the hapless Polish soldiers of 1939 - the first heroic victims of the conflict - to American airmen, knights of the modern age, as well as the French commandos of D-Day and the British troops who fought in the Lybian desert.

The soldiers of five nations are covered in these pages: Poland, France, Great Britain and her Commonwealth, the Soviet Union and the United States.

The wide diversity of he uniforms depicted here follow the evolution of the military dress in a conflict which began with weapons and uniforms that were sometimes more than 20 years old, such as in Poland, through to the perennial silhouette of the American GI.

Only an exceptional team of specialists, researchers and collectors could compile such a significant work crammed with a wealth of informations and colours.

1939-1945 POLISH FORCES

POLISH LIGHT MACHINE

The 1936 Pattern denim tunic is made of khaki-dyed linen that faded quickly to a light tan. The turndown collar and the shoulder tabs are plain. The tunic has four pockets with buttoned flaps and one row of metal buttons down the front. The buttons bear the 1927 Pattern national eagle.

The helmet is made chrome nic molydnenum alloy sprayed with dark o green 'salamane paint with ad powdered cor reduce glare. leather lining has same type of pad as the 1916 Gern 'Stahlhelm' and chinstrap fastens v a flat hook fitting ins a rectangular m eyeh

By Jan Rutkiewicz

AT the end of World War 1, Poland regained her sovereignty, and to empha-size the change, issued her army with new uniforms. In 1935, the Polish soldier was re-equipped with an olive green uni-form to which a denim suit was substituted for the summer months. This little known outfit is described here.

The tan leather, single-pronged 1936 Pattern belt is standard to all ranks and holds the light MG's special ammo carriers of sturdy khaki canvas. The front carriers are larger and have greater capacity (two 30-round magazines) while the smaller side carriers hold only one magazine and have been designed so as not to hamper movements. Interestingly, the carriers are reinforced with steel corners, the carrier flaps are fitted with a strap which slips though a rectangular opening.

Close-up of individual equipment. Displayed on the Pattern 1933 haversack whose markings and straps can be seen clearly: the wide-necked aluminium water bottle and the issue blackened metal folding spoon and fork set. Like the canteen, most metal items were painted and had stamped markings. At, top right, an extra magazine carrier, worn slung across the back.

Pictures: Lech Alexandrowicz. Article written in co-operation with Hieronim and Przemyslav Kroczynski.

GUNNER, SEPTEMBER 1939

 weight of
ipment is evenly
ead, thanks to the
ckened leather 'Y'
ps connecting
front ammunition
ches to the back
he belt. Various
es of harness -
uding French
dels - were also
ed to Polish
ces.

The 7.92mm Browning light machine-gun was adopted in 1928 and officially known as RKM wz. 28. Thanks to its fluted barrel, the weapon could be used in the light machine-gun role. The bipod, front sight hood and finned barrel are noteworthy.

The belt supports the haversack which is suspended in the same way as the German Army model by three straps fitted with a metal hook. Made of waterproofed linen, the haversack can also be worn across the shoulder; its flap is secured by canvas straps with plain buckles. The entrenching tool is carried in a leather holder suspended from the belt.

 French-
de RSC/ARS
mask is
ried in a
tangular
ersack of
ki drab
vas with a
toned
ngular flap.
 is worn
ng on the left
e, over the
oulder.

 1936
tern trousers
made of
ki linen and
like the
ge ones.
y are
hered around
ankles by
vas gaiters
h two metal
tons.

 1934
tern
onailed boots
e screwed
 rather than
vn on - soles
ing better
tection
inst damp.

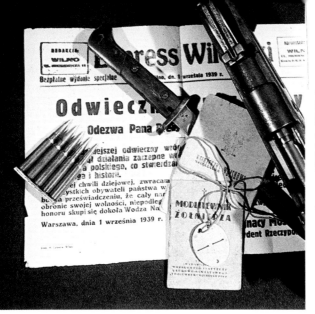

POLISH INFANTRYMAN

The 1931 Model steel helmet is sprayed with drab olive green 'salamander' paint to which powdered cork was added while still wet for a non-reflective finish.

Displayed on the 1 September 1939 special edition of the *Wilno Express* featuring the declaration by the the President of the Polish Republic are: a Model 98A 7.9mm Mauser rifle (Karabin) with the Radom Arsenal markings etched on the breech; the 1927 Model bayonet with the WP (Wojsko Polskie or Polish Army) inscription and the manufacturer's name 'Perkun' at the base of the blade; a five-round clip, a prayer book edited by the military chaplain's department; a pay book and a split ID tag.

The 'Kurtka' tun standard to all Po ground forces. Mac khaki wool serge shoulder tabs - plai privates - sport the insignia. The flaps o four pockets, the fro the tunic and shoulder tabs have alloy buttons, stam with the 1927 Pat Polish national ea

By Jan Rutkiewicz

ON 1 September 1939 at dawn, shots rang out on the German-Polish border – the harbingers of a cataclysm that would become known as World War 2 and claim millions of lives. Inadequately armed, the Polish soldier plodded off to war, stifled in his woollen uniform and burdened with more than 30kg of equipment. He had to walk over dozens of kilometres, in both attack and retreat, but resisted until early October when he was overwhelmed by the Germans and Russians who had turned treacherously against Poland on 17 September.

The locally-manufactured Model 1927 bayonet is slipped into the tan leather frog (also compatible with the German, French and Polish models that were issued to Polish forces). The bayonet is strapped in German fashion to the entrenching tool carried in a fawn-coloured leather holder. The grainy leather ammunition pouches contain ammo clips, each holding 15 Mauser cartridges supplied in cardboard boxes. Displayed on the infantry service manual are a 1924 model fragmentation grenade and the grenadier badge.

The single-pronged 1936 brown belt is made of raw or patent leather. It supports two sets of triple cartridge pouches identical to the German 1909 model and holding two five-round clips of 7.9mm ammunition each.

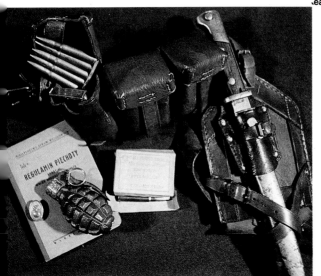

1937
del straight
sers are
in the same
h as the
c and
hered
und the
es by
rt, woollen
ees. The
k leather
4 Model
e boots
e leather
es and are
d with
ded soles
forced by
cleats and
plates.

Left and above.
The 1932 Model 'Tornister' pack is made of thick tan canvas fitted with cotton straps and linked to the ammunition pouches. External cargo includes the mess tin, the greatcoat or the wool blanket (worn horseshoe fashion around the pack).
The pack holds one issue shirt, underpants, spare socks, two handkerchieves, one towel, one pair of laces, the rifle cleaning kit, a sewing kit, an individual shelter quarter and victuals (reserve ration, biscuit and coffee bag).

Left, centre. The 1933 Pattern haversack of waterproofed drab linen is slung over the shoulder by a strap or clipped to the belt. It contains the 0.8 litre bottle, filled with water or ersatz coffee, a salt bag, a bar of soap, towel, toothbrush and toothpaste, plus one small hand grenade. The French 1932 Model gasmask is worn on the right side and carried in a drab linen bag (another model, the French-made RSC was also on standard issue to Polish forces.)

Below. The 1937 Model 'Czapka' (soft cap) was made of drab wool cloth and sported an eagle badge embroidered in silver-grey cotton thread on a wool backing. The officer model was made of gabardine. The aluminium wide-necked water bottle was manufactured in the Swiatovid plant at Myszkow whereas the spoon and fork came from the Grabski plant at Lodz. Next to the cigarettes and lighter, a snapshot of soldiers in walking-out dress topped off by the stiffened, square-topped cap.

The authors wishes to thank Messrs H and P Kroczinsky, Alexandrovicz, Kazimierczak and the Kolobrzeg Museum.

11

POLISH UHLAN

By Jan RUTKIEWICZ

CONTRARY to a persistent romantic myth, Polish cavalrymen armed solely with lances never hurled themselves at German tanks in 1939. No accounts of such suicidal charges appear in official records of the Polish Campaign and this tale is totally unfounded. In fact, the 40 Polish cavalry divisions had discarded their colourful headgear, lances and pennants when they set off for war to defend their homeland. In addition to their Mauser 98 carbines and sabres, the Poles were armed with 16 Browning light machine-guns, 12 Browning heavy machine-guns and four 37mm anti-tank guns.

In the early hours of the conflict, the lethal UR 7.92mm anti-tank rifle was issued to the cavalrymen who, according to Polish cavalry instruction books, '*dismount for combat as horses are exclusively used as a means of conveyance*'.

On 1 September at dawn, the cavalrymen defended stubbornly their western border positions, from Danzig to the Tatra mountains. After the fall of Warsaw, they sought shelter in neutral countries or fought on with the French Army. To break through the German and Russian ranks, however, they charged in the same way as their ancestors had in their celebrated 1812, 1831 and 1920 actions.

Throughout its distinguished history, Polish cavalry did charge, but always for freedom and never against tanks! ❏

The composition includes a plain 'American style' forage cap (made of serge for rank and file and superfine material for officers). The 1934 Pattern sabre is standard issue to the cavalry and has a brown leather knot. The pay book belongs to a cavalry sergeant, displaying his photograph, and provides the backdrop for the Grodno-based 23rd Uhlan Regiment other ranks badge next to a 'Czapka' galvanised eagle. Above left: a divisible, 1938 Pattern ID tag, a sporting military badge and the grenadier qualification badge. To the right, a Mauser cartridge box and field dressing.

The cut of the khaki serge 1936 Pattern tunic was standard to ground forces with four unpleated patch pockets sealed by rectangular, buttoned flaps.

All buttons are galavanised and stamped with the 1927 Pattern eagle. The shoulder tabs indicate the rank of Cavalryman 1st Class.

The single-pronged, brown leather 1936 Pattern belt supports the standard brown, grainy leather ammunition pouches connecting to brown leather braces (French, Austrian and German leather braces were also issued).

The 1919 khaki serge breeches often had canvas (leather for officers) inner leg reinforcements.

Rigt. The linen haversack holds the water bottle, dressing kit, rations and a hand grenade. It is suspended from the belt and hangs over the hip. The Polish-made 1932 gasmask is carried in a canvas bag slung over the right shoulder.

The *Karabinek WZ 98a* carbine is the locally-made version of the famous German cavalry weapon.

The 1927 Pattern bayonet is slipped into a leather frog, itself strapped to the entrenching tool in German Army fashion.

The fawn-leather high boots have unstudded soles. Shown here is one of the numerous types of spurs issued to Polish cavalry.

Below.
Displayed on a Warsaw Ordnance Survey map: a plotter (one of the many types on issue), a compass, a ruler and binoculars. In the centre: an officer's fob watch.

POLISH TANK CREW

The square-topped 'chapka' with the distinctive armoured forces' orange band is displayed on an officer's commission (*Patent officerski*) signed by Marshall Pilsudski. The eagle is of the 1919 Pattern while the star indicates the rank of lieutenant. The 1924-37 Pattern Armoured Corps officer's dagger can be seen next to the parade dress 1928 Pattern belt.

The 1919 Pattern helmet (*Heln* based on the Adrian model with the peak replaced by t leather padding. Painted kha had no bad

LIKE France, Poland underestimated the crucial role tank formations would play in future conflicts and dismissed the intensive militarisation of her neighbours as sheer propaganda. In the prewar years, Poland's war industry was still in the making and, for psychological and financial reasons, the Poles were reluctant to boost their armour as they felt this could only be achieved at the expense of their deep-rooted cavalry tradition. Initially equipped with FT-17 Renault tanks obtained from France in 1919-20, Polish armoured forces had to wait until 1932 for the first licence-built Vickers 7 TP to roll off the assembly lines. In 1937, the 7.9mm machine-guns of these vehicles were superseded by 37mm guns. At the outbreak of the war, the establishment of Polish armoured forces stood at 200 combat vehicles while the Wehrmacht fielded 2,569. As for the Russians who would soon pounce on the hapless Poles, they had no fewer than 4,000!

French influence is conspicuous in the 'Adrian' helmet and the black leather coat worn by this 1939 Polish NCO who wears the traditional cavalry square-topped 'chapka' with colour band, black and orange collar flashes and high boots (the officer's model had spurs). Officers also retained the particular rank titles of the cavalry.

An ordance survey map of Warsaw provides the setting for miscellaneous items on issue to Polish armoured forces: a torch with a switch for morse code messages and notes on transmissions (a similar model is shown on the right in its folded configuration). The manufacturer's name (Granat in Warsaw) and the WP (Polish Army) markings are noteworthy. These markings also appear on the regulation binoculars produced by the H. Kolberg plant, as well as on the compass and the fob watch and chain.

The brown leather (*Pas Glowny*) h single-pronged, b rectangular buckle a cross s Manufactured ir Radom ordna factory, the 1935 9mm pistol is carrie a brown holster secured by a pl leather cord. weapon was issued to field offi and N

A
Pictures:
Alexandrowicz.
author wishes to t
Hieronim
Przemyslav Krocz
for their co-opera

PTEMBER 1939

1936 Pattern double-breasted leather
t coat was designed for air and tank
s and motorised forces. The
r is lined with black cloth. The
indicating the rank of Second
enant, appears on the
ovable black cloth shoulder
buttoned near the collar. The
an sleeves are fitted with
tening straps around the cuffs.
er the leather coat, the standard
plain-collared officer tunic is worn
a khaki sweat rag keeps the
k from chafing.

container for
rench-
ufactured
/ARS
ask is slung
the shoulder
webbing
.

cuffed, brown leather
tlets.

cloth 1919 Pattern
ches (*Bryzesy*).

black leather 'English
' high boots
cerski) are fitted with
aps. Rank and file
nnel were issued
black leather,
ailed ankle boots.

The corporal seen on the
right is clad in the same way
as the lieutenant but for the
tunic worn under the leather
coat and the three crimson-
piped silver rank insignia
worn on the shoulder tabs.
Goggles are suspended
around the neck (several
models were on issue in
1939).

Stiffened
leather
binocular
case.

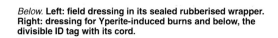
Below. Left: field dressing in its sealed rubberised wrapper.
Right: dressing for Yperite-induced burns and below, the
divisible ID tag with its cord.

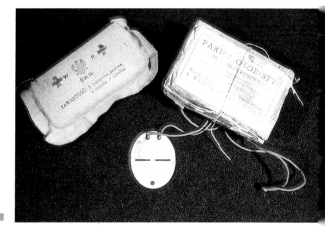

POLISH FORCES IN SOVIET SERVICE, 1943-194

By Jan Rutkiewic
Pictures: Lech
Alexandrowicz

Infantryman, summer 1944. His headgear is the typical Polish soft 1937 Pattern 'Czapka', manufactured in tan serge by the 'Krasni Voin' (red warrior) plant in Moscow. The 1936 Pattern 'Kurtka' (shirt tunic) was also made in the Soviet Union and features Russian-style tan serge shoulder tabs. The metal buttons are stamped with the 1943 Pattern Polish eagle. The 1943 Pattern triangular collar tabs are blue and yellow (traditional Polish infantry colours since 1815). The 1935 serge trousers are tucked into standard Soviet high boots. The man is armed with a PPSh 41 submachine-gun fitted with a drum magazine holding 71 rounds. A spare magazine is carried in a canvas pouch suspended from the belt. Troops issued with 'Avtomat' (Russian for submachine-guns) were known as 'Avtomatchiki' (lack of equivalent expression in Polish led to these men being designated as 'Fizylier').

A female member of the 'Emilia Platter' Battalion in autumn 1943. The dark blue beret sports the 1943 Pattern Polish eagle. Like her Soviet counterparts, the woman wears a 1943 Pattern 'Gymnastiorka', cut in tan cotton with stand and fall collar . Soviet buttons and Polish tan serge shoulder tabs with corporal rank badge complete the garment. In action the 1943 Pattern faded tan breeches were preferred to the regulation dark blue skirt. The high boots, the belt and the pouches for the three submachine-gun magazines are standard Soviet Army issue.

N August 1943, the Soviets began to raise military units from those Poles who had been detained in the USSR ever since eastern Poland had been invaded by the Red Army in 1940. Initially placed under the command of Maj-Gen. Berling, Polish forces fought in the western USSR and eastern Germany, contributing to the capture of Dresden and Berlin in the closing stages of the war.

A Polish infantryman, autumn 1943. Of Soviet manufacture, the 1940 Pattern helmet is adorned with a 1943 Pattern Polish eagle stencilled on the front. The 1936 Pattern greatcoat is made of light tan cloth also of Soviet origin. Its six buttons, stamped with the Polish 1943 Pattern eagle, were painted khaki. The ankle boots are Russian, as well as the puttees, available in various shades of blue cotton or wool. Personal equipment includes a canvas and leather belt, an ersatz ammo pouch and a small 'Myeshok' haversack. Carried on the back, it has a shelter-half strapped to it like a horseshoe, as well as the entrenching tool. The weapon is a DP1927 light machine-gun with a drum magazine holding 47 7.62mm cartridges.

Infantry second lieutenant in summer 1944, with a Soviet-made soft 1944 field Polish 'Czapka' in tan cloth adorned with a 1943 Pattern metal eagle. The 1943 Pattern 'Kurtka' tunic and trousers are made of tan cloth. The Soviet-style stars on the shoulder tabs were issued only to junior officers and indicate the rank. The Cross of Gallantry is pinned above the left chest pocket. Personal equipment includes a Soviet 1935 Pattern Sam Browne belt with 1935 Pattern cloth holster suitable for both the Tokarev 33 and the 1895 Nagant handguns. Equipment is completed by a canvas map folder and 6 x 30 binoculars. The weapon is a PPSh 41 submachine-gun fitted with a curved magazine.

1939-1945 FRENCH FORCES

By François
VAUVILLIER

FRENCH INFANTRYMAN, MAY 1940

IN 1940, the uneven distribution of modern kit resulted in French infantrymen taking varying in appearance, as evidenced by our reconstruction of a typical 'spring 1940 Poilu' kitted out in the latest 1935 equipment but still wearing the early type of greatcoat.

Helmet: general issue helmet, made of manganese steel and painted khaki. The applied insignia on the front is the 1937 Pattern flaming grenade showing that the

gasmask was fastened by a waist strap.

The 1939 Croix de Guerre has been awarded to the soldier and is worn on the chest.

Officially, the greatcoat had two rolled shoulder straps to keep the equipment straps from slipping but many soldiers did without altogether. Only the right one is worn here (on the shoulder where the rifle is carried). Officially each man should have had two rolled straps Although the 1920 Pattern greatcoat was on regular issue in 1940 soldiers were often seen wearing the number one model on active duty. This coat was piped in madder red and adorned with bright gilt buttons but instructions issued on mobilisation specified that the buttons were to be subdued to make them less conspicuous. The 1938 Pattern double-breasted greatcoat overlapped to the right and had a double row of six khaki-painted buttons down the front. At the outbreak of the war, collar flaps were being introduced to conceal the regimental cypher.

The 1935 Pattern personal equipment was made up of linked items: ammunition pouches were buttoned to the front, pack straps secured ato the top of the pouches. The bag of the ANP 31

The infantryman is armed with a 1916 Pattern rifle. This view shows that the 1935 Pattern haversack was carried on the same side as the 1915 Pattern cruciform bayonet (partly hidden by the greatcoat). According to regulations, the water bottle was worn on the right to keep it from rattling against the bayonet. The introduction of the MAS 36 rifle altered this practice and led to the arrangement being reversed (the water bottle was worn on the left and the haversack on the right).

1918 Pattern puttees and Pattern 1917 hobnailed ankle boots.

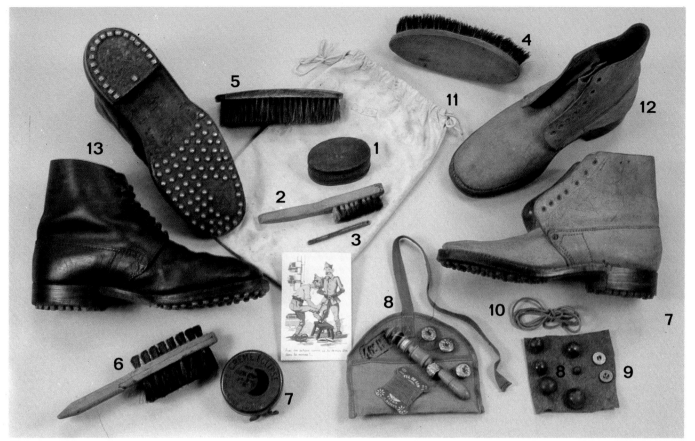

Above.

MAINTENANCE AND CLEANING KITS.

Most items had remained unchanged since the Great War although efforts were made to adjust the kit to each man's requirements. To maintain his rifle, each man was issued with a grease box (1), a brush (2) and a brass pull-through (3) to clean the barrel of his gun. A general use brush (dual function model for shoes) was issued to take care of personal kit. A set of brushes for more specific use was distributed among three men (5 and 6). In the field, use of shoe polish was replaced with grease, resulting in ankle boots retaining natural leather colour (7). Made of khaki cloth, the sewing kit (8) contains a set of needles with thimble, thread and bodkin, four skeins or spools of thread (three khaki and one unbleached). The button set (9) had six khaki uniform buttons (4 x 20mm and 2 x 15mm), two shirt buttons (bone or porcelain) and two white underpant buttons. Spare shoelaces (10) were part of the kit but were carried in the 1935 Pattern upper knapsack for more immediate use. The kit was kept in the lower bag. A lower knapsack containing spare clothing was issued but not included in the marching order (11).

Below.

UNDERWEAR AND DRESSING KIT

In September 1939, French infantrymen were issued with two unbleached cotton cretonne underpants, two shirts with a matching 1935 Pattern khaki tie for each, one woollen pair of socks (1) for winter, one cotton pair of socks for summer, two khaki cloth handkerchiefs (2), and a set of 1932 Pattern braces (3).

Comfort underwear consisted of a 1936 Pattern flannel binder of white worsted wool (4), and thin Pattern 1936 Jersey jumpers replacing the tunic in the field pack. The 'Q' staff provided two towels (5) and a bar of soap (6). For his personal care, the 1940 Poilu had to supply his own dressing kit, unless he was one of the lucky owners of the 'Trousse du Soldat ' (soldier's grooming kit) presented to troops by Gibbs, a toothpaste manufacturer (7). This kit contains toothpaste (8), a shaving brush (9), fine soap (10), and a 'Piccolo' razor kit in its seemingly indestructible khaki steel box (11). Finally, items which helped to make life more comfortable in the field: a small unbreakable folding mirror in its cloth sheath (12), 'Baume Français' skin ointment (13), frostbite ointment supplied by the Medical Corps (14), and a makeshift folding mirror (15).

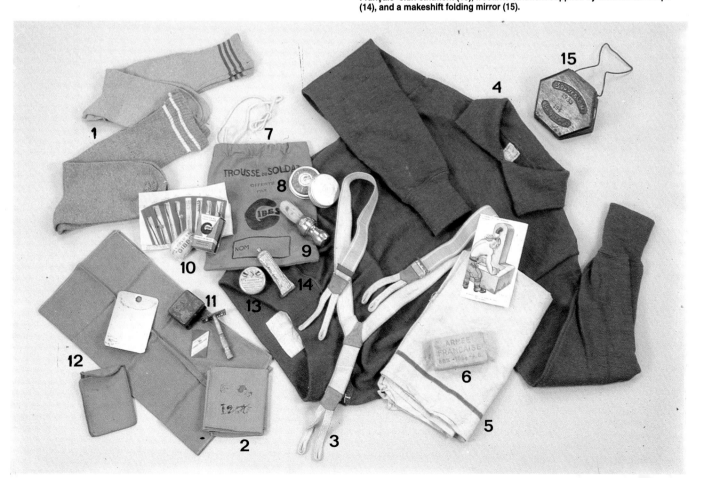

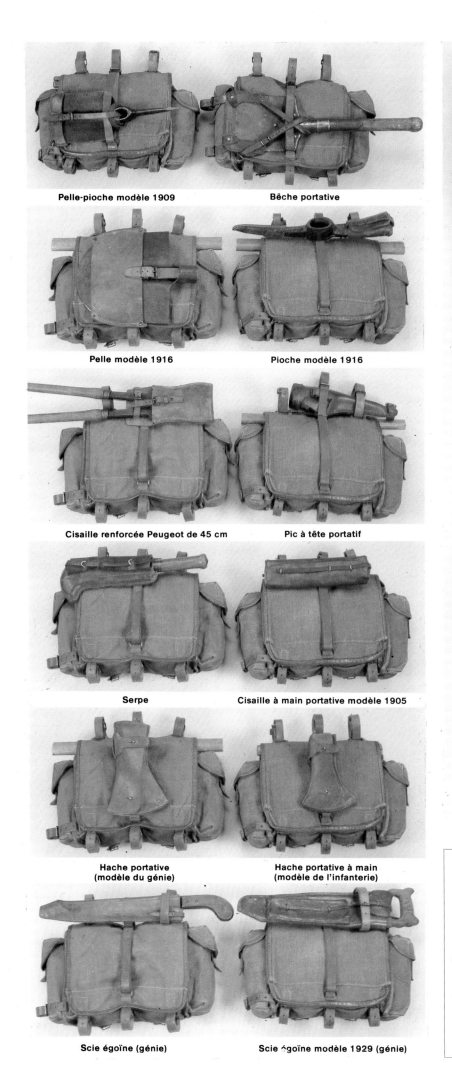

Pelle-pioche modèle 1909

Bêche portative

Pelle modèle 1916

Pioche modèle 1916

Cisaille renforcée Peugeot de 45 cm

Pic à tête portatif

Serpe

Cisaille à main portative modèle 1905

Hache portative
(modèle du génie)

Hache portative à main
(modèle de l'infanterie)

Scie égoïne (génie)

Scie égoïne modèle 1929 (génie)

LOWER PACK CONTENTS

Used to carry the items not needed in combat.

Bottom layer: a brush (for clothes or boots). A set of three brushes was shared among three men.

Middle layer: a shirt, underpants, a pair of socks, a handkerchief, a tie.

Top layer: a sewing kit, a towel and a bar of soap.

MAIN PACK CONTENTS

Carried at all times by the soldier, the main pack contains all the paraphernalia the soldier will need in combat:

Bottom layer: grease box and weapon cleaning tool (wrapped in a rag) and iron rations.

Middle layer: the khaki Jersey jumper (unless worn by the man) and the folded shelter half. The tent accessories (poles, pegs and strings) issued to troops deployed in the north-eastern sector, were discarded following the operational procedure of 6 December 1933 only to be reintroduced on 23 September 1939. When included in the equipment, the half-blanket is secured under the pack flap.

Top layer: a bar of soap, spare shoelaces and a forage cap.

Side pockets: various loads such as: spare magazines, extra ammunition, VB grenades or six hand grenades.

HAVERSACK CONTENTS

Side pockets: light machine-gun magazines and accessories.

Main pocket: mess kit, mug, fork, knife, tin opener and fresh rations.

ANP 31 GASMASK HAVERSACK

Gasmask ANP (*Appareil Normal de Protection or individual protection mask*) in its own carrier with **accessories:** tubes of sodium chloride, spare eyeshield in a paper wrapper, 35M-type filter (fitting the end of the rubber hose).

Left.
Winter configuration with woollen 'tour de cou' (tube-like neck protection of knitted material). The double-breasted 1938 Pattern windjacket (more commonly known as 'DLM windjacket') has a wide rounded front and removable khaki wool serge lining. As the wide collar can be turned up, as shown here, the regimental patches are not worn on the collar but on top of the sleeves (here for the 7e GRDI). In April 1939 buttoned cloth flaps were introduced to cover the sleeve patches.

1935 Pattern motorcyclist helmet wi' pressed metal grenade badge on th front (issued to all cavalry units wi' the exception of armoured ca regiments). The 1935 Pattern goggl have rubber rim

Originating from North Africa, the 'chèche' (long scarf) was worn in summer as a protection against wind and dust and replaced in winter by the woollen 'tour de cou'.

Peacetime
4e RDP
insignia.

Standard infantry equipment consisting of three 1916 Pattern ammunition pouches, with tan leather belt and braces.

Note: the standard field uniform (khaki cloth tunic, breeches, puttees, shirt and tie) is worn under the 1938 Pattern oversuit. For bad weather, side-car passengers were issued with a 1935 Pattern hooded coat of khaki cloth.

By François VAUVILLIER

AFTER two years of experiments, the French Cavalry issued its rifle motorcyclists with a two-piece windproof oversuit far better suited to their duties than the 1935 Pattern.

Made of thick, watertight canvas, the model was introduced in 1938 and consisted of a double-breasted windjacket with matching reinforced trousers. The 1938 Pattern windproof oversuit was widely distributed during the 1939-40 period among the motorcycle squadrons of DLM (Divisions Légères Mécaniques or light mechanised divisions), DLC (Divisions Légères de Cavalerie or light cavalry divisions), GRDI (Groupes de Reconnaissance de Divisions d'Infanterie or infantry division recce groups) and GRCA regiments (Groupements de Reconnaissance de Corps d'Armée or Army Corps recce groups).

1935 Pattern motorcycle gloves which could fit over woollen gloves in winter.

The waterproof 1938 trousers have a fold-down front with two pockets. Access to the uniform pockets is gained through two slits. The trousers have inner leg canvas reinforcements and ankle straps. Theoretically, from 1939 onward all French Army canvas items were stamped in black ink with an 8cm grenade-shaped marking (faintly visible here under the slit). This marking was repeated on the sleeves of the windjacket and stamped on all canvas jackets and coats.

Standard
1917 ankle
boots.

CYCLIST, 1939-1940

MAS 36 rifle, slung at the lower rifle band and fastened to the belt by a leather fitting.

...te: 1892 ...6 carbines ...en replaced ...S 36 rifles ...GRDI and ...CA units. ...opers ...ued with ... former ...rried their ...yonets on ... left.)

...e ANP 31 ...smask) ...versack is ...ng over the ...oulder and ...tened around ...e waist by a ...bbing strap.

Rigth.
Khaki cloth standard pattern sidecap adorned with non-regulation 6e Cuirassiers round patch, and worn here with 1938 Pattern neck protector.

In extreme weather, a Pattern 1938 fur lined undergarment was worn singly or under the windjacket. With elasticated cuffs of khaki knitted wool, the sheepskin garment was adjustable thanks to a canvas half-belt with back buckle. Stripped of its half-belt and improved by the addition of a large fur collar, this garment became popular as the 'canadienne' of Norwegian Campaign fame. (Loaned by 'Le Poilu', P. Bouchery collection.)

Miscellaneous items. At the bottom of the helmet dome is a 1938 Pattern 'shock absorbing' pad fastened under the lining by laces (on exclusive issue to motorcyclists).
Metal box for the 1935 Pattern goggles with elasticated bands. Also shown: 1935 Pattern gloves with calf leather lining, tightening straps and typical cuff markings.
Under the gloves, the 1938 Pattern 'tour de cou'.
Insignia include 7e GRDI collar and sleeve patches and cap flash of 5e Cuirassiers.
'Troupes' cigarettes, second-choice 'Gauloises' on exclusive sale to troops.
Mounted troops 1923 Pattern belt fitting suitable for MAS 36 and 1923 Model rifles.
Fragment of canvas uniform showing the regulation black grenade stamp.

1935 Pattern water bottle with long strap.

FRENCH GENERAL OFFICER

TYPICAL FIELD DRESS
The general wears the field dress képi of khaki serge, enhanced only by an oakleaf braid chinstrap and two silver stars (repeated on the cuffs).

Pattern 1926 helmet with p◼ leather chinstrap and silver ◼ According to regulations, gen◼ helmets were devoid of a pre◼ badge indicating the arm of se◼ (such as the infantry gre◼ shown here) but this was ◼ disrega◼
The 1939-40 French fo◼ greatcoat was their ◼ distinctive garment and i◼ issued to all ranks, from priva◼ generals. This general, how◼ has opted for the raglan sle◼ coat in preference to the li◼ and shorter model also issu◼ gen◼

Dark◼
lea◼
glo◼

IN October 1939, the full parade dress with madder red breeches was discarded for the duration of hostilities. Only French generals were allowed to wear the khaki serge full dress - except for a few minor differences - as the 'tenue de jour' (N° 3 full service dress), the 'tenue de travail' (N° 4 service dress) and the 'tenue de campagne '(N° 5 field dress).

In the French Army, all men are equal and the short stick (bottom left picture) is banned whenever the officer is with troops under arms! A longer 'trench' walking stick, however, could be substituted for the sabre when the field dress was worn.

Bottom left. **According to regulations, the map folder can be suspended either from the saddle for mounted officers or from the left side of the belt with its upper edge flush with the tunic. This general is no stickler for regulations as is evidenced by his folder being carried higher than regulations and on the opposite side to the revolver. The banishing of the sabre from the field dress leaves the right hip free, which explains this more practicable arrangement.**

FIELD DRESS, 1939-1940 by Richard de Filippi and François Vauvillier

929 Pattern field
ce tunic has the
lled 'aiglon' collar,
dard to officer
s before the
duction of the
collar (both were
andard issue in
). For full service
s configuration, the
lder tabs of the
ary service and
dresses are
ced with gilt
ed tabs.
garment has silver
above the cuffs,
ral officers' gilt
ons
ars of
ls.

Compatible with all service dresses and often worn on field duties such as inspections or parades under arms, the embroidered kepi was a colourful subsitute to the khaki model.

Above. Close-up of miscellaneous equipment on issue to French generals: folder (the smaller, non-regulation model on the right was in widespread use); khaki sidecap with dark khaki piping and two stars; two kepis; dark tan gloves. In the foreground: short stick, walking stick, spurs, bootjacks, cigar holder, sabre strap and visiting-cards sent by General Franchet d'Esperey and General George.

Below. Pondering a possible counter-attack. The ANP 31 gasmask is carried in a haversack and is as much part of a general's equipment as that of a private. The same applies to the 1935 Pattern water bottle, on standard issue but hardly ever used by officers.

TYPICAL SERVICE DRESS

Regulation dark tan Sam Browne belt with 'ham-shaped' holster for 1892 pistol. By 1940 this model was obsolete but had lost none of its elegance!

Dark brown leather high boots could be worn with N° 3 dress (those shown here are hand-made Lobbs) whereas khaki puttees, leggings or boots were compatible with the N° 4 and 5 dresses only. But wartime regulations allowed generals to chose the footwear they felt best suited their duties and that was preferable for long walks such as laced and strapped boots (for instance when inspecting troops at the front).

light 'mastic-
ured' regulation
ches with
ching leather
forcements
ame regulation
e for officers in
. When N° 3 or 4
ses were worn,
reeches could be
aced with straight
ki trousers
ned with dark
ki piping and
le bands down
outer seam. This
el was
usively issued to
erals (officer
ches had only
large band).

FRENCH COMMANDO

Left. One for the family album! Before the crossing, this commando had his picture shot by a Southampton photographer. The full insignia are displayed here: 1er BFM (Bataillon de Fusiliers Marins or Marine battalion) cap badge, introduced in 1944 and worn in British fashion pinned to the beret above the left eye. The 'France' and 'N° 4 Commando' embroidered shoulder titles are worn above the Combined Operations patch on the sleeves of the battledress blouse. The enamelled FNFL (*Forces Navales Françaises Libres* or Free French Naval Forces) insignia can be seen on the chest pocket.

...he cap badge was usually removed before action.

The brown canvas jerkin for Bren magazines supplements the 1937 Pattern basic pouches.

ON 6 June 1944, the 1st Battalion de Fusiliers Marins Commandos (Marine Commandos) led by Lieutenant Kieffer stormed the German stronghold at Ouistreham Riva Bella. On that famous day, the prestigious commandos could only be distinguished from other units by their badges and specific equipment.

1943 Pattern light gasmask.

SMLE N° Mkl. rifle.

Left. For the crossing, the Mk II steel helmet is fastened on top of the rucksack, and the ground sheet strapped under its bottom. The water bottle and the entrenching tool are standard.

Studded ankle boots. A rubber-soled model was also issued to shock troops for amphibious operations.

Canvas anklets

'DAY 1944

By Hervé HALFEN

Mk II steel helmet camouflaged with netting and hessian strips.

In order to look stylish, the man has purloined Canadian-made battledress. Identical to the British 1937 Pattern. This garment could be differentiated by its darker colour and superior cut.

Bergam rucksack holding food and ammunition supplies for several days.

1937 Pattern water bottle.

Canadian-made battledress trousers.

Above.
After landing at Colleville beach, this commando has discarded his rucksack and is bracing himself for fighting through the streets of Ouistreham. The light combat order includes basic pouches, two cotton bandoleers, a light gasmask in its watertight olive green haversack and a toggle-rope. The Mk II N°4 spike bayonet is suspended from the belt. The helmet is Canadian-made, as shown by the adjustable chin strap with eyeholes.

Below.
Some evocative items from the 1er BFM (Bataillon de Fusiliers Marins Commandos) displayed on an FNFL standard : a Bergam rucksack of rubberised canvas, a Mk II helmet with camouflage net, a British regulation commando beret with 1er BFM badge, a flute-handled Fairbairn-Sykes commando dagger, an FNFL enamelled badge, a Mills M36 hand grenade, a jerkin for spare Bren magazines and a toggle rope.

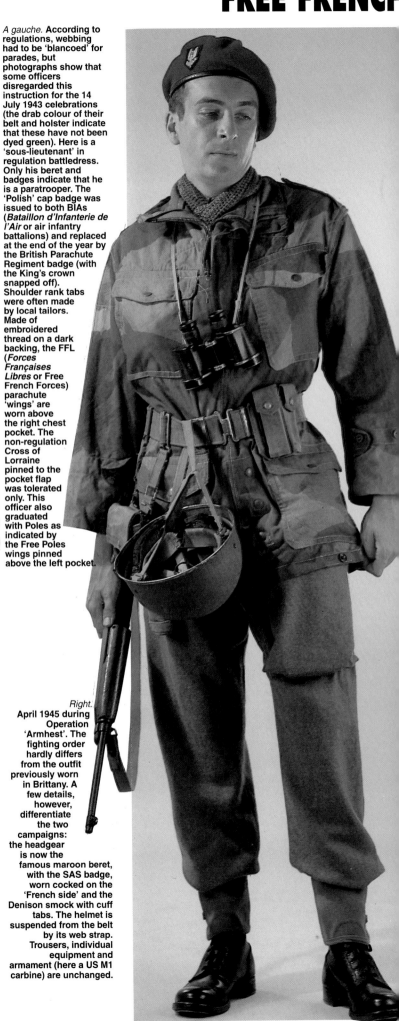

A gauche. According to regulations, webbing had to be 'blancoed' for parades, but photographs show that some officers disregarded this instruction for the 14 July 1943 celebrations (the drab colour of their belt and holster indicate that these have not been dyed green). Here is a 'sous-lieutenant' in regulation battledress. Only his beret and badges indicate that he is a paratrooper. The 'Polish' cap badge was issued to both BIAs (*Bataillon d'Infanterie de l'Air* or air infantry battalions) and replaced at the end of the year by the British Parachute Regiment badge (with the King's crown snapped off). Shoulder rank tabs were often made by local tailors. Made of embroidered thread on a dark backing, the FFL (*Forces Françaises Libres* or Free French Forces) parachute 'wings' are worn above the right chest pocket. The non-regulation Cross of Lorraine pinned to the pocket flap was tolerated only. This officer also graduated with Poles as indicated by the Free Poles wings pinned above the left pocket.

By Denis LASSUS

RAISED in Britain on 20 July 1940 by General de Gaulle, the Free French airborne forces were trained in Britain and the first batch graduated in December 1940. From 1941 to 1945 they distinguished themselves in numerous operations and fought in Brittany and the Ardennes (1944). They were deployed in the Netherlands when the war ended.

Right. April 1945 during Operation 'Armhest'. The fighting order hardly differs from the outfit previously worn in Brittany. A few details, however, differentiate the two campaigns: the headgear is now the famous maroon beret, with the SAS badge, worn cocked on the 'French side' and the Denison smock with cuff tabs. The helmet is suspended from the belt by its web strap. Trousers, individual equipment and armament (here a US M1 carbine) are unchanged.

PARATROOPER, 1944-1945

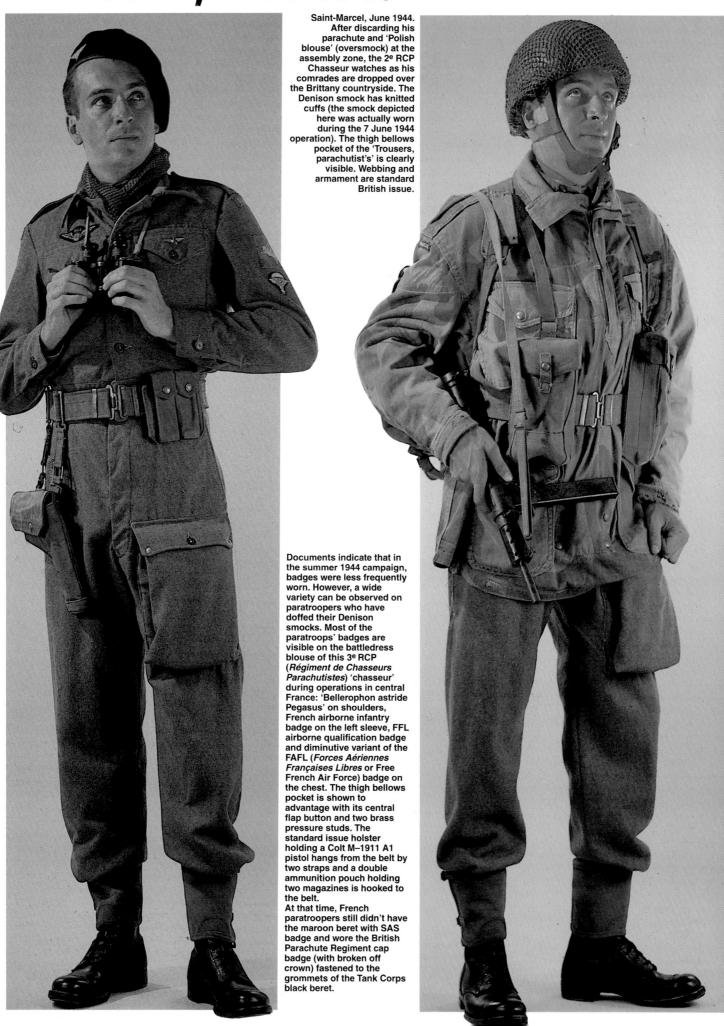

Saint-Marcel, June 1944. After discarding his parachute and 'Polish blouse' (oversmock) at the assembly zone, the 2e RCP Chasseur watches as his comrades are dropped over the Brittany countryside. The Denison smock has knitted cuffs (the smock depicted here was actually worn during the 7 June 1944 operation). The thigh bellows pocket of the 'Trousers, parachutist's' is clearly visible. Webbing and armament are standard British issue.

Documents indicate that in the summer 1944 campaign, badges were less frequently worn. However, a wide variety can be observed on paratroopers who have doffed their Denison smocks. Most of the paratroops' badges are visible on the battledress blouse of this 3e RCP (*Régiment de Chasseurs Parachutistes*) 'chasseur' during operations in central France: 'Bellerophon astride Pegasus' on shoulders, French airborne infantry badge on the left sleeve, FFL airborne qualification badge and diminutive variant of the FAFL (*Forces Aériennes Françaises Libres* or Free French Air Force) badge on the chest. The thigh bellows pocket is shown to advantage with its central flap button and two brass pressure studs. The standard issue holster holding a Colt M–1911 A1 pistol hangs from the belt by two straps and a double ammunition pouch holding two magazines is hooked to the belt.
At that time, French paratroopers still didn't have the maroon beret with SAS badge and wore the British Parachute Regiment cap badge (with broken off crown) fastened to the grommets of the Tank Corps black beret.

MOROCCAN GOUMIER

The eyes of this 'old sweat' reflect his nostalgia for the sun-scorched undulating dunes of his North African homeland. Although 'Goum' officers answered to the Colonial Office and were thus issued with light blue sidecaps, the lieutenant depicted here has opted for the dark blue, 'banana' shaped model, with light blue crown and piping. This headgear was regarded as more practicable and fashionable than the old, plain 'square' caps. The gilt piping of the rank insignia is repeated on the chest as is the custom on garments without shoulder tabs. The unit insignia is sewn on the left sleeve so that the unit could be identified when the helmet replaced the sidecap. The 'chèche' (long African scarf) was part of every 'African' soldier's kit and is worn here around the neck.

By Pierre BESNARD and Patrice BOUCHERY

AFTER being integrated with the 1st French Army, the 1st, 2nd and 3rd Groups of Moroccan 'Tabors' fought to secure the passes that barred the way to Colmar during the 1944 Alsace campaign. Unaccustomed to the extreme weather of eastern France, the 'Goumiers' froze to the bone in sub-zero temperatures. Many suffered from frostbite and had to be evacuated. The sunny beaches of the Provence landings were a long way behind!

Only the headgear, insignia and gloves are French Army issue. Everything else, such as the comfortable Mackinaw short coat (initially meant as winter protection for drivers) is American. Its wool lined collar is typical of the earlier models.
Suspended from the M-1936 webbing belt are a leather M-1916 holster for the M-1911 A1 handgun and web double pocket ammunition pouch.

The woollen M-1937 trousers are tucked into M-1938 canvas leggings and worn with issue ankle boots.

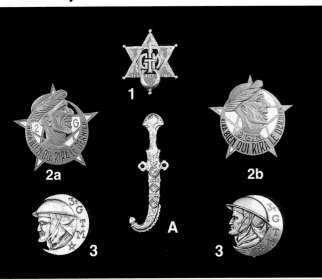

'GOUMS' INSIGNIA :
Top : Standard badge.
1 : 1st Moroccan Tabors Group.
2 : 2nd Moroccan Tabors Group.
3 : 3rd Moroccan Tabors Group.

...t from the French
...rsack containing the
...1931 gasmask worn on
...eft hip, the man is
...ely issued with
...rican kit. The presence
...orld War 1 equipment
...teworthy and quite
...al of American
...lies to the 'French
... of the Liberation'.

The 'Goumier's' most distinctive garment was the 'jellaba', a traditional, locally-made striped gown. Originally, the width and colours of the stripes differentiated the various units but this practice was dropped as the 'Tabors' moved farther away from North Africa. After the 1944 Provence landing, a simplified version was introduced and issued to all units. This consisted of a 'muraille' pattern of ochre, brown and black stripes with a green piping down the front and along the sleeve seams. The gown was worn over the standard US combat uniform.

Both M-1903 Springfield and US17 rifles were on regular issue to Tabors. The bayonet is carried in an M-1910 scabbard.

Consisting of a loose woollen skein, the 'khiout' is the traditional headgear of Tabors who usually had their heads shaved. For better protection against the cold, this Tabor has wrapped his head in the 'chèche', and topped it off in typical fashion with his steel helmet. Contrary to a widespread belief, 1st French Army 'Goumiers' never had British helmets but US M-1917A1s.

A 'chèche' provides the backdrop for Tabor paraphernalia including: a US Mk I trench knife (Moroccan Tabors were the only French World War 2 troops issued with this obsolete weapon). Regarded as fragile and fitted with an awkward attachment system, the pressed steel sheath was replaced by the M-6 scabbard initially meant for the USM-3 knife. Officer sleeve insignia with light blue piping, metal crescent and stars (below). This insignia can be differentiated from the non-regulation model above thanks to its gilt piping which replaced the colour of the arm of service and gilt embroidery. The dark blue lieutenant's sidecap with light blue crown and piping is displayed on an Arabic-French conversation manual. In late 1944, a new sidecap was introduced and worn concurrently alongside the two others meaning that, for a while, the unit had three different regulation field service caps! The piping was phased out after the war.

...dard US Army
... wool and
...er gloves.

...1-1942 field
...sing pocket
...an M-1918
...ch knife in an
...eather
...bard are
...pended from
...webbing
...17 cartridge
...and braces.

...ope better
...the harsh
...atic
...ditions, the
...tional 'naïls'
...dals) and 'tariouines'
...ted stockings) have
... superseded by
...rican ankle boots
... overshoes for
...ection against snow
...mud.

On issue to shock troops only, the khaki knit wool cap is one of the hallmarks of the battalion. The model shown here is an American 'Beanie' (Wool knit cap, M–1941) with its peak removed.
As Colonel Gambiez who led the battalion during the capture of Toulon (prior to commanding the Groupement de Choc) recounted in *The Liberation of Corsica*:
'*In action, the "chasseurs" discarded the French armoured forces helmet, in favour of the woollen cap after removing its cardboard peak reinforcement. This resulted in comfortable headgear that could be folded down over the ears in cold weather.*'

Simplified US garments were worn 'Chocs' during the su operations. Hard insignia were us shown by this se 'mopping up' in Toulo combat uniform cons an American wool shi rolled up sleeves a M–1943 herringbon trousers. His o topped off by an M peakless wool kn Embroidered in thread on a dal backgrour 'sergeant is horizonta the shirt prewar s f garr a s

Standard US issue webbing equipment (pistol belt and braces). The weapon, however, is a British Sten submachine-gun. Spare magazines are carried in the US trousers' cargo pockets.

A mere four months after its creation, the 'Bataillon de Choc' took part in the liberation of Corsica (September-October 1943) and was then successfully deployed in Elba in June 1944. On 20 August, the battalion landed in Toulon, southern France, where it fought for five days. As a general reserve unit, the battalion followed the advance of the 1st French Army and took part in the September 1944 campaign in Alsace. The 'Chocs' didn't lay down their arms until the invasion of Austria in May 1945.

By Denis Lassus

Cut from a US 1942 Pattern service coat, this type of blouse remained on French Army issue until the early 1950s. The blouse shown here belonged to a sergeant and can be dated back to 1945-46 thanks to its 'Bataillon de Choc' and 'Rhin et Danube' sleeve insignia. The '1939-45 Croix de Guerre' ribbon and the unit insignia are respectively pinned above the left and right chest pocket flaps. A single chevron was sometimes sewn on the left sleeve as a substitute for the shoulder tab rank insignia. Previously made of unbleached linen, the lining of the late-war beret is of black material, while the leather reinforcement tab fitting behind the cap badge had yet to be introduced.

DE CHOC', 1944-1945

Even though operational reports specify that the dark blue beret was hardly worn before late 1944, it seems that it was issued shortly after the unit was posted to Dijon in September. Indeed, at times, the wearing of the beret was the only way to differentiate the 'Chocs' (who didn't) and their sister unit, the Commandos de France (who did). During the Battle for Germany however, the beret often replaced the wool knit cap. In the same way as the Algerian War model, the beret was made up of several pieces of dark blue cloth and had a black leather band with adjusting cord.

The look of the 'chasseurs' hardly changed since the June 1944 landing (the unit had been redesignated as 1er Battaillon de Choc in January 1945) but during the 1944-45 winter campaign, American overcoats and jackets were worn over standard US outfits. Badges and insignia, however, appeared more frequently on combat uniforms as typified by this 'adjudant-chef' (warrant officer): on his M-1941 Field Jacket, he has sewn the shoulder title created in Algeria for the battalion and consisting of 'Bataillon de Choc' lettering embroidered and piped in yellow thread on a dark green backing. The slip-on rank insignia appear on the shoulder tabs as often was the habitual practice in the 'French Army of the Liberation'. Hardly ever worn in action during the late 1944 campaigns, the cap badge became more conspicuous as the end of the conflict neared.

The severity of combat didn't preclude humour as shown by this brochure released just after the war and recounting in waggish style the exploits of the battalion. Illustrated with cartoons, the brochure faithfully mirrors the mood prevailing in the unit. Miscellaneous battalion insignia are displayed above the brochure and include: the shoulder title, embroidered in yellow on a dark green backing; the unit insignia; the cap badge and American airborne wings. The odd, light tan background is provided by the reverse side of an US M-1941 Field Jacket. Both 'Bataillon de Choc' and 'Groupe de Commandos de France' used to wear this garment inside out, a practice that can be explained by two reasons: firstly, the colour of the jacket was regarded as too light and conspicuous in the field while the shade of the lining was a better match for the US khaki trousers. Secondly, these garments were relatively fragile and hard to replace. This practice helped 'chasseurs' to reduce wear and maintain their smart appearance. Interestingly, this custom was observed in Corsica and in the Vosges.

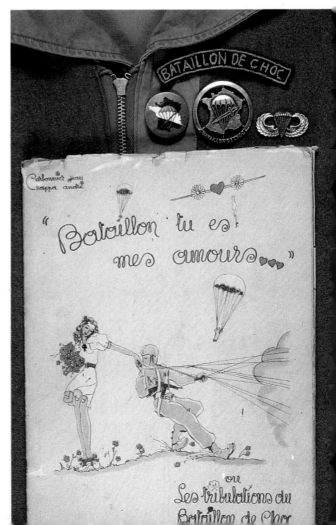

"Bataillon tu es mes amours..."

ou
Les tribulations du
Bataillon de Choc

Left.
The airborne infantry insignia on the helmet and the 'mounted troops' cartridge belt differentiate this 'chasseur parachutiste' from 1st French Army and American units deployed in Alsace. His American 'Buckle boots' are also typical as few units were issued with this type of footwear in late 1944. The boots were frequently worn with overshoes, most commonly known as 'snow boots' among French units.

Right.
A lieutenant in walking out dress with US issue 'coat, parachute jumper, 'trousers, parachute jumper', 'boots, parachute jumper' and French Air Force dark blue side cap. The US airborne qualification wings are worn above the airborne infantry insignia (but could replace the 1er RCP regimental badge).

Opposite left.
A para in full jump outfit. The US M-1 helmet sports the French tricolour on the right side (a common practice among the French Expeditionary Corps in Italy and later adopted by the 1st French Army). The 1918 Pattern cartridge belt is worn here, although the almost identical 1923 Pattern was also issued. By the same token, the scabbard of the M-3 knife could have been an M-6 leather model instead of the plastic M-8 shown here. The embroidered French airborne infantry wings include a bird of prey above the 'wings'. Paras of all ranks favoured the locally embroidered insignia they obtained from army tailors.

Opposite, right.
1er RCP soldiers were also issued with American mountain troops kits for a mission in the Balkans which never got past the planning stage. The equipment, however, was retained and used during the 1944-45 winter campaign in eastern France. This 'chasseur' has tucked his reversible green/white parka into his mountain trousers, a common practice in the regiment. The 'beanie' (wool knit cap), woollen scarf, mountain boots and ski gaiters complete the set worn in extreme winter conditions.

By Denis LASSUS

DESCENDED from the 1940 Airborne Infantry Groups and answering to the French Air Force until August 1945, 1er RCP (Régiment de Chasseurs Parachutistes or parachute regiment) was raised in 1943 from the CIA N°1 (Compagnie d'Infanterie de l'Air) and created in Algeria from former members of 601e and 602e GIA (Groupement d'Infanterie de l'Air).
Waiting for the resumption of fighting, the volunteers trained in Algeria with prewar materiel and uniforms until re-equipped by the Americans in 1943.

ROOPER, 1943-1945

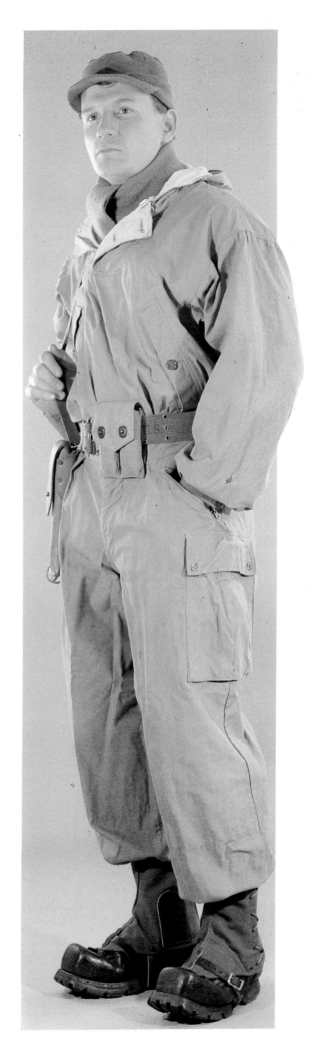

By Denis LASSUS

Left. Adopted in North Africa by the 'Groupe de Commandos de France', the dark blue beret remained that unit's distinctive headgear until the 'Bataillon de Choc' also selected it during the battle for the liberation of France. Made of several pieces, the headgear is broadly based on the British General Service Cap, but features the same black leather band as the maroon and black berets. Initially, it could be worn in British or French fashion (cocked either to the right or to the left) and only later did regulations dictate that it be worn cocked to the left only. Badges were forbidden but berets often sported a Cross of Lorraine or American airborne wings.

RAISED about a year after the 'Bataillon de Choc', the battalion-sized 'Groupe de Commandos de France' (French Commando Group) operated along the same lines and ethos as its sister unit. The commandos played a clandestine part in the Provence landing where they operated as 'Détachement Special' under the command of Major d'Astier de la Vigerie. Early in November 1944 the group intervened in the Vosges campaign and fought as front line troops until victory. In January 1945, the unit became the 3e Bataillon de Choc and was consolidated within Colonel Gambiez's 1er Groupement de Bataillons de Choc.

In February 1945, the French commandos and other allied troops paraded through the streets of Colmar, eastern France, to celebrate the liberation of that city. Overcome by the jaunty springtime atmosphere - or out of defiance to the chilly weather - the commandos decided to march in shirt sleeve order to shame the other soldiers who paraded in greatcoats and field jackets. However, as the men of the 1er Bataillon de Choc also wore dark blue berets, the two main 'choc' units could only be differentiated by their specific insignia.

Left. The *'COMMANDO DE FRANCE'* title and star (inherited from the 1940 'Corps Francs' shock infantry units) are embroidered in madder red thread on a dark blue background. Some titles however had no pipings. Sewn on the left shirt sleeve are: a self-made commando title (without piping, on a dark blue background) and an embroidered star without piping, on a black backing. The piped insignia shown here have a dark blue background. Left: American airborne wings Gallicised thanks to the addition of a brass Cross of Lorraine. This type of insignia was worn on or above the flap of a chest pocket or alternatively on the cap.

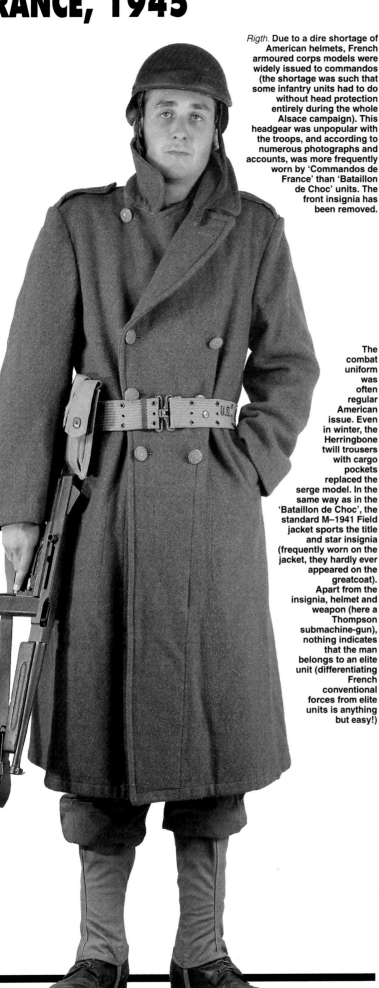

Rigth. Due to a dire shortage of American helmets, French armoured corps models were widely issued to commandos (the shortage was such that some infantry units had to do without head protection entirely during the whole Alsace campaign). This headgear was unpopular with the troops, and according to numerous photographs and accounts, was more frequently worn by 'Commandos de France' than 'Bataillon de Choc' units. The front insignia has been removed.

The combat uniform was often regular American issue. Even in winter, the Herringbone twill trousers with cargo pockets replaced the serge model. In the same way as in the 'Bataillon de Choc', the standard M–1941 Field jacket sports the title and star insignia (frequently worn on the jacket, they hardly ever appeared on the greatcoat). Apart from the insignia, helmet and weapon (here a Thompson submachine-gun), nothing indicates that the man belongs to an elite unit (differentiating French conventional forces from elite units is anything but easy!)

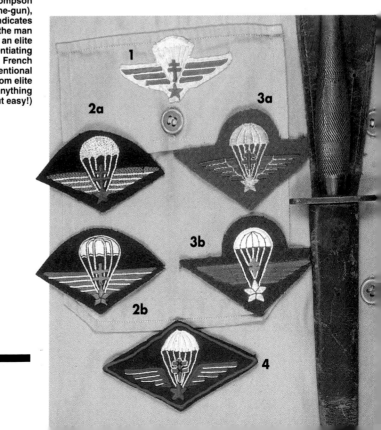

Above. Pictured on the front of a light khaki shirt (US officer model): 1st Commando insignia with blue star (a commando unit was on average, the size of a company). In summer the light tan shirt was widely used, although such light garments were certainly more frequently seen in North Africa than in Germany. The insignia shown below are: 2nd Commando (2a and 2b) white star and 3rd Commando ('Commando Lourd' or heavy commando) red star. The embroidered insignia (3a) was French-made and standard issue after the 1944 landing. The piping and symbols of 2b and 3b insignia have been embroidered in orange thread for unknown reasons. Number 4 insignia with red piping originates from North Africa.

1939-1945
BRITISH AND
COMMONWEALTH
FORCES

BEF INFANTRYMAN, 1939-1940

By De Bello-Nord and
Philippe CHARBONNIER

MAY 1940: on a beach near Dunkirk, a British NCO from the 2nd Glosters (48th South Midland Division) is on his way back to Britain after fighting a last rearguard action at Bergues.

This warrant officer enlisted just after World War 1 and rose through the ranks of his regiment to become Company Sergeant Major. The running battle with the Germans has had no effect on this veteran: his personal equipment is still consistent with regulations - no small achievement for a soldier in retreat! His typical uniform and kit convey a good impression of the British infantryman's appearance in the first half of the European conflict.

The weather is hot and the soldier has undone the collar of his battledress blouse. In the left hand picture, the large patch pocket and the wide cut of the trousers are shown to advantage. The gasmask haversack and the gas cape strapped to the top of the large pack are in the 'alert position'. The regulation issue jack knife dangles from the webbing belt. Suspended from the end of the webbing braces, the enamelled water bottle in its felt cover hangs on the right hip. It could also be carried in the haversack. The handle of the mug is slipped into one of the haversack straps.

The Mark II steel helmet is a derivative of the Mk I introduced during the Great War. The main differences are the oilskin lining, the shock absorbing rubber pads and the elasticated chinstrap.
Consisting of a woollen blouse with matching trousers, the 1937 Pattern early battledress was evolved in the 1930s. The battledress blouse has five buttons down the front and its loose collar is fastened by two metal hooks. The waist is gathered into a 3in wide belt. Extending from the latter on the left side is a 9in long strap fastening with a metal buckle at the side of the waist to allow for adjustment. Patch pockets are placed on each breast. The only insignia is the brass rank badge on each sleeve.

The battledress trousers are cut moderately wide in the leg and gathered around the ankles by a buttoned tab. High up on the left leg is a deep patch pocket with buttoned flap. On the right leg is a smaller, pleated patch pocket for a field dressing packet. Ordinary side pockets are inserted and there is a single hip pocket with buttoned flap at the back on the right hand side. Usually worn with white elasticated braces, the trousers have four buttoned tabs to hold the webbing belt.
The M1937 equipment is made of cotton webbing. The different items are linked together in an attempt to spread their weight evenly. Suspended by both the belt and the braces are a pair of 'basic pouches' that accommodate a cotton bandolier of 50 rounds and two hand grenades each.
The heavily hobnailed 'ammunition boots' are made in pebble-finish blackened leather. The web anklets with internal leather reinforcement are fastened by two buckled straps. The soldier is armed with a bolt-action Rifle N°1 Mk III* Short Magazine Lee Enfield of .303in calibre and bayonet N°1 Mk.I, both introduced in the Great War.

The Coloured Field Service Cap was worn with the General Officer's Service Dress and Battledress with 'mess dress and for other informal occasions'. This dark blue headgear with scarlet crown has gold braid welts on the cap flaps, and on the front and back seams. The rank is indicated by the side bullion insignia while the front of the cap is adorned with two small buttons featuring the same design. Manufactured from khaki material, the single-breasted officers' Service Dress jacket displays the rank badges of General. The Staff Officers' (unassigned to any specific service or branch) Service Dress has scarlet felt gorget patches, embroidered with gilt oak leaves and topped with a general's button. The medal bars on the chest represent (from left to right):

The General is cla his Officers' Servi Dress and Officer Breeches, Mounte Pattern, of drab tw with matching bu strappings. Cut as lounge coat to the with a back seam, dress jacket is loc the chest and sho but fitted at the wa Manufactured fror khaki material, it h two pleated breas pockets and two l pockets below the

waistline o each side. three-point pocket flap were faster four gilt bu adorned wi badge of ra (these butt were repea reduced si the pockets shoulder ta the cap an field servic cap). The S Browne bel brown. The privately purchased brown lace boots were manufactu Lobb's of London. Un his right ar General ca bamboo sti and a Prox raglan rain from a rang designed b Burberry's highy prize British offic The khaki Service Dre cap with sc band and general ran badge has crown.

- Order of the Bath (awarded in 1938)
- 1918 Distinguished Service Order.
- 1914-15 Military Cross.
- British War Medal.
- Victory Medal (with palm).
- General Service Medal.
- 1939-45 Star.
- Jubilee of King George V Medal.
- Crowning of King George V Medal.
- Norwegian War Meda

I N 1940, French and British troops were dispatched to Narvik to block the German advance towards the Norwegian iron ore deposits. Commander of the force, Major-General Pierce Joseph Mackesy, led a reconnaissance mission to Narvik but in the face of German opposition, chose to set up his headquarters at Harstad on the neighbouring Lofoten islands.

The General was accompanied by an advanced detachment of Scots Guards when he sailed from Britain on board the cruiser HMS Southampton. Arriving in Narvik on 15 June 1940, Mackesy decided against a frontal attack and, together with the Norwegians, evolved a strategy to outflank and capture the city. General Mackesy, however, didn't see his plan come to fruition: recalled to London, he was replaced by General Auchinleck on 14 May. Two weeks later, Narvik was occupied by French and Norwegian forces.

1940

By Richard de FILIPPI

...e General has just... Buckingham ...ace after a staff ...nference presided ...r by King George ...The peak of the ...rlet-banded khaki ...e features a double ...y of oakleaf braid. ...tching the Officers' ...vice Dress, the ...users have ...turn-ups ...d are ...n here ...1 ...wn ...her ...shoes. ...e sabre ...bbard is ...tected ...a brown ...her ...ath.

Buckingham Palace, March 1939: Major-General Ian Hay Beith, Public Relations Officer has just attended the King's rising. When on official duty, Generals carried their swords from the Sam Browne belts. The stiff pattern Service Dress Cap has patent leather chinstrap and peak adorned with a double row of oakleaf braid.

Bottom.
Forage Cap with scarlet band and double row of oakleaf braid on the peak, made of patent leather like the chinstrap. This headdress was manufactured by White, tailors of Jermyn Street in London. Right, the khaki serge Service Dress Cap, Soft Pattern, with scarlet band and brown leather chinstrap is shallower than the Stiff Pattern model. This cap carries the label of Herbert Johnson, a prestigious tailor of New Bond Street in London. The badges of rank on the three caps (crossed sword and staff in a laurel wreath topped by the royal coat of arms) are embroidered in gilt bullion on a dark blue backing (the sword blade is embroidered in silver thread). The Coloured Field Service Cap in the centre was made by Gieves, another famous tailor of Savile Row in London. The shoulder tab rank insignia are made of brass. Major-General Mackesy was promoted to the rank of general after the end of the war as shown by the crossed sword and staff topped with a star and a crown. The distinctive red colour of the Staff Corps to which the two officers belong is showing through the crown. The letter 'R' stands for 'Reserve'.

HOME GUARD VOLUNTEER, 1943

As shown by his shoulder insignia, Harold Pettigrew belongs to the 28th Territorial Battalion from Hampshire. From top to bottom, his insignia are: the 'Home Guard' title in white lettering on a chocolate brown backing, and the black letter on a greenish backdrop indicating his county of origin - in this case 'H' for Hampshire. The letter was replaced by a red rose in certain territorial companies. Filling his pipe in front of the Union Jack, Harold Pettigrew typifies the indomitable spirit of the British people protecting King and Country.

By Franck BACHMANN

Middle Wallop, 5 September 1943, early evening. Harold L. Pettigrew was about to pull down the steel shutters of his chemist shop when, suddenly, a dark shadow loomed across the sky, skimming low above the rooftops.

Pettigrew's heart leapt into his mouth: although shortsighted, he had immediately identified the silhouette of one of the Nazi raiders that carried out hit-and-run forays over the British isles. The tell-tale rattle of the engine and the plume of smoke issuing from the cowling left hardly any doubt about the aircraft's fate. As quickly as posssible, Harold donned his Home Guard equipment, jumped onto his bike and pedalled off into the twilight as fast as his legs could go.

Standing guard by the downed raider, Pettigrew has donned the regulation groundsheet, supplied to the Home Guard from 1941 onwards, as a replacement for the shoddy serge cape on exclusive issue to the Volunteers. The Mark II helmet hangs from its chinstrap over the right shoulder (the helmet's grainy green finish indicates a wartime production model).

The odd mixture of individual equipment consists of a utility brown leather belt, double cartridge carriers of various shades of green (holding two clips each, this type of pouch was issued to non-infantry units), web braces, 1908 Pattern large pack with brown leather utility straps and a Mark I bayonet.

The gas mask is worn high on the chest in the 'alert position'. Home Guard personnel often wore a mixture of leather and webbing anklets (both identical; the leather model was on specific issue to the Home Guard). A British Army Lantern Electric Traffic N°2 is slipped on the bayonet of the N°1 Mark III* rifle, a weapon that progressively replaced the US 17 model issued earlier in the conflict (and incompatible with the rimmed .303 cartridges). As a souvenir of this memorable day, Harold has tucked into his belt the German airman's side cap he found in the wreck.

In this composition, the General Service Respirator is displayed next to an ersatz ammunition pouch made of hardened cardboard and leather (on specific issue to the Home Guard), and the individual field dressing. The tubes of Ointment Anti-Gas N°5 were carried in the gasmask haversack.

Below.
1944: Snug and warm in the back room of his shop, Harold enjoys the traditional 'five o'clock' tea steaming in an enamel mug. Like a seasoned veteran, he cleans up his N°1 Mark III* rifle with the pull-through and oiler (on the crate next to the Field Service Cap) carried in the weapon's butt. The 1940 Pattern Battledress trousers have no buttoned tabs at the waist and are held up by regulation braces.

He only had one thought on his mind as he dashed to the crashsite: at long last, he would get his 'Jerry'!

'Dad's Army'

Raised on 31 July 1940 from Local Defence Volunteers groups, the Home Guard was made up of male personnel aged from 16 to 65 ineligible for one reason or another for regular service. The Home Guards were entrusted with the defence of British territory, releasing young fit men available for regular service while at the same time reassuring the population.

LDV home guardsmen were volunteers who trained after work or at weekends. By the end of 1940, their ranks totalled about 500,000 men, organised like standard territorial units and answering to the Chief of Staff of the Home Forces.

Affectionately known as 'Dad's Army', this jaunty, motley force included people from all walks of life - students, pensioners, Great War veterans, shopkeepers and VIPs. The Home Guard gave sterling service by fulfilling obscure but necessary duties such as the surveillance of key locations (factories, harbours, marshalling yards etc) while also being tasked with a more glorious and thrilling mission: the capture of German airmen forced down over British territory. ❐

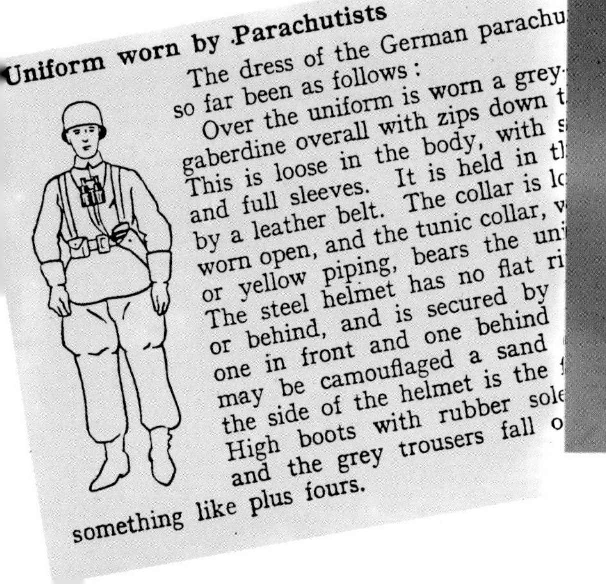

Uniform worn by Parachutists
The dress of the German parachu...
so far been as follows :
Over the uniform is worn a grey...
gaberdine overall with zips down t...
This is loose in the body, with s...
and full sleeves. It is held in th...
by a leather belt. The collar is lo...
worn open, and the tunic collar, w...
or yellow piping, bears the uni...
The steel helmet has no flat ri...
or behind, and is secured by...
one in front and one behind...
may be camouflaged a sand...
the side of the helmet is the...
High boots with rubber sole...
and the grey trousers fall o...
something like plus fours.

47

Above.
One of the numerous instruction manuals unofficially obtained by enthusiastic members of the Home Guard: how to overpower German paratroopers and aircrew.

Belove.
An aerial chart of Britain found in the cockpit of a German aircraft provides the backdrop for this composition. A Field Service Cap adorned with the Hampshire Regiment plastic badge. The metal cap badge at the bottom was issued in the early stages of the war. Home Guardsmen had to sport their county's cap badge, but veterans often disregarded official instructions and wore their traditional headgear and badges instead. The carefully crafted cap has two General Service buttons on the front.
The paper form was used by Home Guardsmen to specify the nature of wounds suffered on duty and includes first aid-tips on the obverse side. The Defence Medal was awarded in wartime to civilian and military personnel who had served for three years at home or six months overseas. By 1943, it had been awarded to numerous Home Guard volunteer.

Spick and span and frozen at attention, Harold Pettigrew stands alert during an inspection by King George VI. Shown to advantage here, the 1940 Battledress Blouse and Trousers were not introduced until 1942 and before, the Home Guard had to make do with the Denim outfit. Embroidered in red thread on a greenish backing, the chevron indicates one year of service. The brown leather holster on the belt carries a flexible link saw. Pettigrew has carefully polished his hobnailed ankle-boots before the ceremony although the grey, woolknit anklets somewhat detract from his warlike attitude.

48

BRITISH NAVAL BEACH COMMANDO, 1942

ON 19 August 1942, the major amphibious raid on Dieppe by Anglo-Canadian troops ended in dismal failure in spite of the gallantry of the attackers. Of the 5,000 men brought ashore, the Allies lost 3,350 killed and wounded, 28 tanks and a number of larding craft. The lessons learned, however, proved invaluable for later Allied amphibious assaults.

Left and right. **Raised in early 1942, the Royal Navy Beach Commandos were trained to guide in the landing craft needed to bring ashore an infantry brigade with its support units, vehicles and supplies. A beach commando unit was made up of a principal beach-master, three beachmasters, six assistant beachmasters, three petty officers, six leading seamen, 18 able seamen and 39 seamen. The units were subdivided into three groups, each attached to a battalion. Put ashore just after the first wave, the beach commandos' task was usually complicated by enemy fire as they set up the beacons to guide in the landing craft (radios, torches and loudhailers were also used). The beach commandos' duties included firefighting and the recovery of beached and scuttled barges. They also silenced strongholds, cleared beach obstacles and often fought it out like infantrymen.**

The beach commando's uniform was a mixture of army and navy equipment that included : the battledress (blouse, trousers and gaiters) worn alongside typical navy gear such as the grey blue helmet and the dark blue, woollen round-necked jumper which reached below the blouse. On the left sleeve (above) can be seen a petty officer's anchor and crown insignia. The three stripes sewn under it indicate 13 years of 'undetected crime' (good conduct). Worn exclusively on this uniform, the shoulder title of 'Royal Navy' is in white lettering on a black backing. The combat order has been reduced to waist belt, braces with brace attachments, holster and ammunition pouch. Consisting of a white rubberised cloth tube in a sturdy blue canvas cover, the RN-issue life belt is worn around the wa under the equipment. It was fastened around the neck and the waist by straps and inflated throu the tube with valve seen at the front.

In the picture, the man has salvaged one of the flags Canadians carried in their kits to testify to their country's part in the conflict. Some of these flags were given by wounded Canadians to the inhabitants of Dieppe who tended them.

By Philippe Charbonnier on Bernard Petitjean

Next p
Belonging to the Mount-Royal Fusiliers who landed with the first wave, this sturdy 'Can displays his uniform to advantage. The Mk II steel helmet is covered with cotton netting; Canadian battledress blouse with buttoned collar sports a blue disk above the formation sig both sleeves, indicating that the wearer belongs to the 1st Battalion of the 6th Brigade. personal equipment includes: waist belt, straps, and pouches (to carry rifle ammunition, h grenades, Bren magazines, mortar bombs etc). The Pattern 1907 bayonet in its webbing frog the water bottle are suspended from the belt. The Navy life belt is firmly held in place by webbing. The anti-gas cape is fixed at the back to the braces (oddly, pictorial evidence sugg that no gas masks were worn during Operation 'Jubilee'). Connected to the ammo pouches, haversack straps are worn above the shoulder tabs for quick release. The brown rubber groundsheet is slipped under the haversack flap. The lack of entrenching tool is noteworthy. trousers are identical to the British 1937 Pattern model with two side and one single hip po with a flap at the back on the right side, and one large patch pocket on the left leg. High u the right leg is a small pleated pocket to take the wearer's field dressing packet. There are buttoned belt tabs at waist level, while the bottom of the trouser leg ends are gathered w buttoned tab for easier fitting of the web anklets. The Canadian grainy leather ankle boots leather laces, cleated tips and heels, but no toe-plates; the soles are partly hobnailed. weapon is the 'trusty' SMLE N°1 Mk III*, with its typical Canadian-made yellowish web s
(Petitjean and Le Poilu collecti

CANADIAN INFANTRYMAN, 2ND DIVISION, 1942

THE CANADIANS AT DIEPPE

THE CALGARY REGIMENT

This officer belongs to the Canadian 14th Army Tank Regiment, one of the first Canadian armoured units to be bloodied in the European theatre. The combat headgear adorned with the regimental cap badge is the traditional armoured forces black beret. The Mk II steel helmet was only worn outside the tank. The British type black fibre protection helmet is not shown as it was probably not worn at the time. The colour tab stars indicate the rank of second lieutenant. The second lieutenant rank pips on the blouse's shoulder tabs are embroidered in white and fawn thread. Documents suggest that the Calgary Regiment was the only Canadian unit wearing embroidered shoulders titles (opposite) during the Dieppe landing. These non-regulation insignia were made in Britain. The Tank Regiment insignia (a representation of a World War 1 Mk I) is sewn on the right sleeve to commemorate its affiliation with the British Royal Tank Regiment. The Canadian 1st Army Tank Brigade insignia, showing a black ram on a yellow maple leaf superimposed on a black rectangle, only appeared on the unit's Churchill tanks. The officer's green poplin shirt is worn with a tan tie which shows through the collar which is kept open thanks to vigorous flat ironing. The Light Combat Order individual equipment includes braces which connect to the waist belt by means of metal brace attachments. Identical to the 1937 Pattern British model, the Canadian-issue holster hanging over the right hip was on exclusive issue to armoured forces personnel. A small ammunition pouch is worn on the left. The individual weapon is a British double-action .38 Pistol Revolver N°2. Spare cartridges and a cleaning rod are kept on the holster. The tank commander's hands are protected by brown leather gauntlets. The trousers (with field dressing pocket clearly visible on the upper leg), the web anklets and the ankle boots are standard Canadian issue.

Clad in a light tan canvas overall, this Canadian prisoner is either an armoured forces' officer or a crew member from one of the few Daimler recce vehicles that made it ashore during the Dieppe operation. (ECPArmy)

BRITISH COMMANDO, DIEPPE, 1942

RAISED in June 1940, N°3 and 4 Commandos were the first units of this type ever commissioned in Britain. Their ranks included many Dunkirk veterans.

By Philippe CHARBONNIER

Deployed at Dieppe in August 1942, N°4 Commando recorded one of the few successes of ill-starred Operation 'Jubilee' by destroying the clifftop 'Hess' battery at Berneval

Left.
Completely functional, the design of N°4 Commando's uniform benefited from actual combat experience. For easier identification in combat, the cap comforter replaces the steel helmet. Devoid of insignia, the uniform is the khaki denim suit cut like the serge 1937 Pattern Battledress. The plastic blouse buttons are removable; a face veil protects the soldier's neck while the straight trousers fall over the footwear. The boots have moulded rubber soles which give good grip on slippery decks and allow for stealthy movement (they do not clatter and cannot be confused with German hobnailed 'Stiefel'). Armed with an SMLE and 1907 Pattern bayonet, the soldier is issued with the standard webbing equipment consisting of belt, braces and pouches. The haversack is hooked to the back of the ammo pouches and the toggle rope dangles from the belt. Extra ammunition is carried in cotton bandoleers. The blue RN lifebelt is deflated. *(Bouchery and Coleman Collection).*

Above.
The typical silhouette of a N°3 Commando Bren gunner. At the time, the hallmarks of this unit were the hessian helmet cover with loops, the brown camouflage cream on hands and face, and the 1937 Pattern battledress blouse adorned by black shoulder titles with embroidered white lettering. The man wears a light tropical shirt under the blouse. The anklets and hobnail boots are standard issue. The RN lifebelt is worn under the webbing (belt, pouches, straps and haversack). The personal weapon of Bren gunners serving in the Commandos was the Colt M-1911A1 handgun, carried under the ammo pouch in the standard British holster.
(Coleman and d'Elia Collections)

March 1944. The 5th Division has just landed at Anzio to relieve the 56th Division sent to North Africa for refitting. This corporal is a section leader from the Royal Inniskilling Fusiliers. His combat uniform and equipment are standard British Army issue and include the Mk II steel helmet with camouflage netting, the 1937 Pattern serge Battledress, web anklets and black leather hobnailed boots. The 1937 Pattern individual equipment includes two large chest pouches to carry hand grenades and submachine-gun magazines. The US-made Thompson submachine-gun was often issued to British infantry NCOs fighting in the Italian campaign.

BRITISH INFANTRYMAN, ANZIO, 1944

By Philippe CHARBONNIER

ON 22 January 1944, some 50,000 Anglo-American troops with 5,200 vehicles landed at Anzio on the western coast of Italy without opposition. Forty-eight hours later, most of the troops were ashore but Generalfeldmarshall Albert Kesselring's quick reaction rapidly brought German reinforcements from the north pinning the Allies to the beachhead.

Below.
Insignia of British Units Deployed at Anzio-Nettuno
A - 1st Division. The typical spearhead, symbol of the 1st Corps, to which the 1st Division belonged in 1940 when part of the BEF.
B - 5th Division. The 'Y' stands for Yorkshire, where the unit was traditionally garrisoned.
C - 56th Division. The insignia of this London unit features a black cat, referring to a popular British folk story and a symbol of good luck in Britain.
D - Set of sleeve insignia worn by 43 Royal Marine Commando in 1944.
E - Shoulder titles adopted in 1943 by N°9 Commando. In action, officers could be distinguished by a white strip on the shoulder tabs replacing rank insignia. During the Italian campaign, commandos only wore insignia on walking-out and Number One dresses.

The South African Tank Corps was raised on 29 May 1940 and, for want of heavier vehicles, was issued with locally-made Marmon-Herrington armoured cars at a rate of 36 per regiment. Tasked primarily with recce missions, the SATC units were first engaged against the Italians in Abyssinia and Somalia. Later, they distinguished themselves during the Western Desert campaigns, before commissioning within the South African 6th Armoured Division following the disbandment of the SATC in 1942.

The SATC cap badge is pinned black wool beret. Sporting the design, the metal SATC collar ins is pinned to both jacket l

The typical South African S Dress is made of light khaki gaberdine with a waistcoat p on the right. The metal butto adorned with the South Africa of arms. The shoulder tabs hav rank pips of blackened metal (us all South African forces) ar orange sli distinguishing v teers for ove service. The sleeve adorned pointe facing an small buttons ribbons cate th office been d M Cros brav the the Star the

S M

Early October 1942: a lieutenant from the SATC's 4/6th Armoured Car Regiment, aunit resulting from the amalgamation of the 4th and 6th Regiments. The man is about to attend a staff meeting before Operation 'Lightfoot' (the second battle of El Alamein). His unit formed one of the British 1st Armoured Division's recce groups, as shown by the divisional sign, a rhinoceros, on the sleeves of his officer's jacket.

A member of the South African 1st Armoured car Company, a recce unit of the 1st South African Division. A veteran from the East African campaigns, this soldier is about to return to combat after a period of rest in Egypt in late 1941. For combat and light chores, a black beret (often larger than in British formations) replaces the pith helmet. The Indian-made lightly woven tropical shirt is adorned with the traditional South African orange slip-ons. The divisional sign appears on both sleeves. The ankle boots are already heavily scratched by desert sand and pebbles. Individual equipment is standard armoured forces issue. The handgun is attached to the shoulder by a lanyard. The soldier is seen performing a task vital to tank crews - refuelling - and carries a 'Flimsy', a British-made petrol can not known for its sturdiness.

The Service Dr completed by a l leather Sam B belt, a shirt, a cotton tie and l leather low shoe sunglasses provi indispensible prot for soldiers serv North African cour

**Jacques
IGNON**

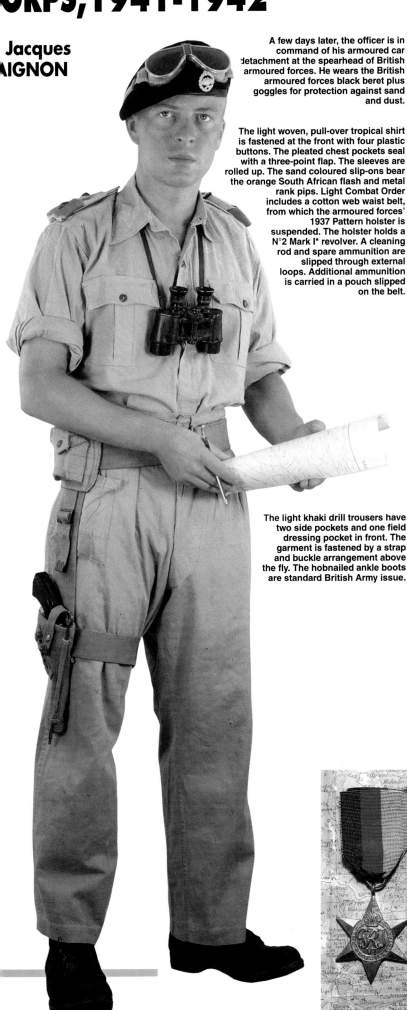

A few days later, the officer is in command of his armoured car detachment at the spearhead of British armoured forces. He wears the British armoured forces black beret plus goggles for protection against sand and dust.

The light woven, pull-over tropical shirt is fastened at the front with four plastic buttons. The pleated chest pockets seal with a three-point flap. The sleeves are rolled up. The sand coloured slip-ons bear the orange South African flash and metal rank pips. Light Combat Order includes a cotton web waist belt, from which the armoured forces' 1937 Pattern holster is suspended. The holster holds a N°2 Mark I* revolver. A cleaning rod and spare ammunition are slipped through external loops. Additional ammunition is carried in a pouch slipped on the belt.

The light khaki drill trousers have two side pockets and one field dressing pocket in front. The garment is fastened by a strap and buckle arrangement above the fly. The hobnailed ankle boots are standard British Army issue.

1941 South African Tank Corps cap badge. The early model carried the 'SATC-SATK' acronyms and did not have the springbok head at the top. The motto 'Ons is' means 'Here we come!'. Above, the Egyptian-made 'cheap' version of the badge and below, the better South African crafted model.

An Italian map of western Africa provides the backdrop for campaign medals awarded to South African forces deployed in this theatre. These medals were actually awarded to Sapper J.P. Pugsley who served with the South African Engineer Corps. From left to right:
- 1939-45 Star: awarded for six months service in an operational zone.
- Africa Star: awarded for spending at least one day in the operational zone (North Africa, Abyssinia, Eritrea, Malta and Somalia) between 10 June 1940 and 12 May 1943.
1939-45 War Medal: for at least 28 days of active service during the conflict. The South African-made version is made of cupro-nickel and, unlike the British version, carries the receiver's name.
South Africa Africa Service Medal: awarded to South African personnel on active duty in Africa before 12 May 1943. Note: The first three medals were awarded to British and Allied forces personnel. (Franck Bachmann Collection).

BRITISH JUNGLE UNIFORMS, 1942-1945

By Robert d'Elia
and Eric Crépin-Leblond

SIMULTANEOUS with their sweep across the Pacific, the Japanese struck the British in Malaya in December 1941. Their advance proved irresistible and, some two months later, the garrison of Singapore commanded by General Percival surrendered unconditionally. The Japanese harried the British all the way to the Indian border before a defence line could be set up and placed under the leadership of Lieutenant-General William Slim, commander of the newly-created XIVth Army. It would take until August 1945 to defeat the Japanese and take back the conquered land.

This study delves into the uniforms of the two British divisions which fought in the South East Asia theatre prior to being consolidated within the British XIVth Army.

The British soldiers who faced the 1942 Japanese onslaught were clad in a two-piece combination of khaki drill short-sleeved shirts and shorts. These garments were worn with solar pith or Mark II steel helmets. British Command soon realised that this combat gear was totally inappropriate for jungle warfare and, when the units were re-created by mid-1942, the men were issued with a new range of combat uniforms far better suited to local conditions. The colour of this new outfit was officially known as 'Jungle Green', a shade that can be best described as greyish green.

Headgear

A new range of headgear was introduced to replace the standard headgear issued to forces deployed in Europe.

The Jungle Drill Field Service Cap. Indian-made, its shape is reminiscent of the standard khaki Field Service Cap. Made of drill cloth, it is lined with unbleached linen with markings inked in black (like all Indian-made garments). These include the manufacturer's name, size and production date.

The Jungle Green Drill General Service Cap. Of Indian manufacture, it is also made of jungle green drill cloth lined with unbleached linen. Almost iden-

Opposite (front and rear view. **Burma, 1944. This Jock from the 1st Battalion, The Cameron Highlanders, found that the 'Slouch Hat' afforded better protection than the traditional 'Tam o' Shanter'. His headdress is adorned with the 2nd Division sign. The Indian-made Jungle Green Battledress with Aertex blouse provides good ventilation. On the shoulder tabs, the brown wool slip-ons sport the regiment's name in black thread. Cut moderately wide for ventilation, the trousers are made of sturdier cotton drill. The trousers legs are gathered around the ankles by puttees, better suited for jungle operations than web anklets, and worn here with standard 'Ammo Boots'. The Scot is armed with an SMLE N°1 Mk III* rifle and a 1907 Pattern bayonet. The pouches hold two light machine-gun magazines, ammunition clips for the rifle and hand grenades. The cotton bandoleer holds extra rifle ammunition.**
Rear view: the man has lowered the brim of his hat to shelter against the driving rain. The soldier is equipped with the Pattern 1937 web equipment, dyed with Blanco N°3 for reduced visibility. Personal equipment includes Basic pouches, small pack with ground sheet folded under the flap, mug, water bottle and bolo. Ill-adapted to jungle warfare, the webbing became heavier when soaked, dried slowly then shrunk and eventually rotted.

Right. **A fusilier from 1/8th Lancashire Fusilier Battalion on guard duty in a rear zone. He wears the Jungle Green General Service Cap adorned with the regimental cap badge along with an Aertex bush jacket that could be worn as an alternative to the battledress blouse for walking-out and under arms duties. The standard trousers are gathered by regulation anklets, and the rifle is the newly introduced N°4 Mk 1* with spike bayonet.**

tical to the serge model, it was introduced in 1943.

The Jungle Green Drill hat. Indian-made and looking like a fisherman's hat, it was issued circa mid-1944.

The Felt Hat. Colloquially known as the 'Slouch Hat', 'Wide Awake' or 'Smasher', the most highly prized and typical headdress among British forces remains the Felt Hat. This khaki drab headgear was actually introduced at the beginning of the century. Soldiers were particularly fond of it as it shielded the eyes from the sun, sheltered the nape against the rain and kept leeches away from the neck. Ventilation was provided by two brown painted steel eyelets placed on either side of the crown. The puggaree (or pagri), a long length of muslin wound around the crown, was originally meant to be soaked with water to cool the head by evaporation. The brown leather chinstrap is fitted with a plain brass buckle. The left side of the brim (the side on which the British soldier carries his rifle) can be raised and kept up by a pressure stud. Arm of service or unit flashes could be sewn on either side of the puggaree or on the upturned brim of the hat. Most of these hats were manufactured in Britain.

The standard steel helmet worn in Burma was the Mark II, painted in various shades of green, sometimes combined into a two-colour scheme for camouflage purposes. Helmets were often covered with thin meshed netting, or the broad-meshed Indian-made net. Green and brown hessian strips were often added to the nets for camouflage.

Uniforms

The standard early 1942 uniform was the khaki drill combination, first dyed 'Jungle Green', but the colour washed off quickly. By mid-1942 Indian manufacturers started producing Jungle Green battledress. Known as Indian Pattern, it included:

The Jungle Green Aertex Battledress Blouse. Broadly similar to the standard denim coverall blouse, it is made of the same light Aertex material used for tropical shirts. The garment has three back buttonholes matching three buttons on the trousers.

The Jungle Green Aertex Bush Jacket. Cut in the same light material, the jacket has four patch pockets and a removeable belt. The jacket could be tucked into the trousers like a shirt. Unit and rank insignia were generally omitted.

The Jungle Green Drill Battledress Trousers. The straight trousers are made of standard drill cloth. They fasten with a five-button fly down the front and are adjusted by two front buckled straps at waist level. Early models had belt loops. It has the same pockets as the serge battledress model, but with a patch pocket to the back of the right side. Six buttons were sewn in pairs inside the tops for braces (which were hardly ever worn). These garments have typical dished embossed metal buttons.

Some garments were also manufactured by local 'Darzi' (or 'Durzi') Indian taylors and variations in cut were not unusual: three-point pocket flaps, trousers devoid of left front pocket, or replacement of the jacket by a shirt.

In late 1944, the war in Europe was drawing to a close and British Army strategists could devote more attention to the Far Eastern front. Troops fighting in this theatre were then issued with a new jungle outfit.

British Pattern Jungle Green Battledress. A new jungle outfit was designed under the auspices of Royal Army Ordnance Corps. Consisting of a cotton shirt and trousers, it was manufactured in two different kinds of material: a denim type of twill and a lighter poplin, both darker than the previous materials. The cut of the trousers was retained. The uniform incorporated a chest 'gas flap' and anti-gas cuffs. Black rubber and brown plastic buttons were used.

Shirt, Jungle. With six buttons down the front, the shirt has two plaited chest pockets with pointed flaps (the shirt pocket has a pen holder). Trapezoid cloth reinforcements are stitched on the shoulders. An anti-gas flap is sewn along the left inner front and fastens onto the other side by three buttons. It must be unstitched before use. The sleeves have anti-gas cuffs. Anti-vesicatory (blistering) chemicals give the cloth a clammy feeling.

Trousers, Jungle. Practically identical to the Indian Pattern, the trousers have a four-button fly, fasten around the waist with two straps. The 'Trousers, Jungle', have four belt loops buttoning downwards (unlike the 1937 Pattern serge trousers). The large pocket has been removed from the left thigh and replaced by a back pocket. The trousers are fitted with drawstrings at the hem of the legs.

War Aid (WA) Uniforms

American manufacturers helped to make up British production problems through the 'Lend Lease' programme. These garments were cut in the typical US herringbone twill (HBT) material and used the same plastic buttons as American 'fatigue' uniforms.

Shirt, Jungle, WA. Basically identical to the British jungle shirt but of simpler design as evidenced by the chest pockets, the shirt

1944: clad in an American-made jungle outfit and wearing a bush hat, this British soldier from the 2nd Infantry Division is on picket duty somewhere in the Burmese jungle. Lightly equipped for the mission, he carries a bandoleer and captured Japanese binoculars in addition to his service weapon. His uniform is the same colour as standard American HBT 'fatigues'.

bears one British and one American-type manufacturer's label.

Trousers, Jungle, WA. Similar to British garments with only the cloth and buckles being markedly different. Interestingly, the regular issue US HBT 'fatigue' hat was also worn by some Tommies. This study shows, however, that most troops deployed in this theatre were issued with Indian-made uniforms. The standard footwear was the black grainy leather ankle boot ususally worn with puttees or web anklets.

Individual equipment and armament

The standard web equipment was the 1937 Pattern 'blancoed' in dark green. As the war drew to a close, a modified Mark IV helmet with removable liner as well as a lighter 1944 Pattern webbing set were designed but unissued. Lighter underwear and various canvas pouches made of green cloth (for sewing or dressing kits) were issued along with talcum powder and insect repellent.

The N°1 Mark III* infantry rifle was the standard service weapon throughout the campaign. Unlike the lighter N° 5 Jungle Carbine which saw use only after the war, the N° 4 was issued in limited quantities. The regular issue machete fitted with a strong steel blade and carried at the belt in a brown leather sheath was on standard issue to soldiers on duty in the jungle. ❏

Right. **Burma, 1945. This soldier from the XIVth Army is shown in the standard British-made jungle combat uniform. By then, the Indian-made jungle jackets and blouses had been superseded by a new shirt-like tunic. The trousers are identical to the Indian model. The Aertex material had been abandoned and replaced with either a sturdy denim twill or a lighter, tightly woven, poplin (like the model depicted here). The standard issue equipment consists of a Mk II steel helmet with Indian-made netting, a SMLE N°4 Mk I* rifle, and a bolo (machete) manufactured in the United States to British requirements. The 1937 Pattern anklets, the webbing and the boots are standard.**

Below. **Rear view of the British-made shirt/tunic showing the shoulder cloth reinforcements for haversack straps and the rifle's sling. Another interesting feature: the access slits and the set of tabs at kidney level probably meant for the gas-cape. Gas attacks were regarded as a real and serious threat in the closing stages of the campaign in the Far East.**

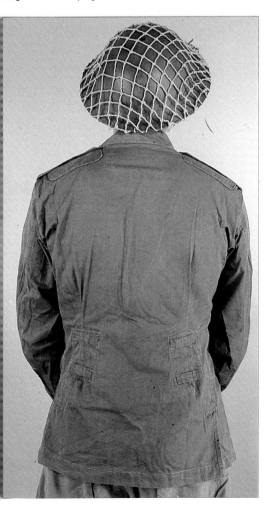

61

RAF AIR GUNNE[R]

Clad in the splendid RAF service dress, this corporal poses for the traditional studio portrait. The basis of RAF flying clothing is the everyday blue-grey Service Dress uniform, consisting of an opened-necked, single-breasted, four-buttoned tunic worn with straight matching trousers. Made of smooth barathea(worsted or worsted and silk) for officers and serge for other ranks, the tunic has four patch pockets; the breast pockets were pleated, buttoned, and had three-point flaps for all ranks. The unpleated straight-flapped skirt pockets had no buttons in the other ranks' version. All buttons were of brass or gilt metal. The nationality of the gunner is indicated by the embroidered title worn on the left sleeve, the cap badge (consisting of the Polish national eagle over the crown of the Kingdom of Poland), and the Polish lapel rank insignia (worn along with British arm 'stripes'). The RAF NCO and other ranks' embroidered eagle badge appears on the shoulder above the commemorative insignia indicating that the man lived in France at the outbreak of hostilities. The Polish observer's badge is pinned above the left pocket flap.

Strengthened canvas parachute straps with quick-release buckles. The parachute was stored away during flight and hooked to the two chest buckles only when required.

During the flig[ht] gunner has donn[ed] bomber crew fli[ght] over his S[ervice] Dress. Dev[eloped] pocke[t] sheepski[n] jacket has z[ips] down the fro[nt] cuffs. M[ade of] canvas, the 'Mae We[st'] preserver fa[stens] with stra[ps] three b[uttons] down the [front] Add[itional] kapok pa[ds] inc[rease] buo[yancy]

Flying personnel's typical items displayed on an aerial chart of the Channel: MkIV B flight goggles, side cap with NCO and other ranks' badge, electrically heated gloves, gunner/observer's log book, the wooden model of a Wellington handcrafted in 1942 during off duty hours; three brevets (far right), and two wartime photographs showing mechanics servicing a Vickers .303 machine-gun(top left) and inspecting a rear turret (centre right).

Te trous[ers] are on[e of] several ty[pes] issued to [flight] crews with li[ned] pockets brass butt[ons]

manufactur[er's] label appe[ars] on the in[side] side of [the]

EARLY 1942, 'somewhere in England', an RAF corporal is about to board a Wellington bomber for a mission over Germany. This rear gunner is a Polish volunteer who has found his way to Britain after fighting in the Polish and French campaigns. Determined not to give up the struggle, Poles arrived in Britain as early as 1940 and more than 14,000 of them served in the ranks of the RAF.

RITAIN 1942 — By Frédéric FINEL

sheepskin collar
e raised for
ort and kept up
a buckled strap.

Close-up of the headgear: the leather-mounted Mk IVB flight goggles have painted metal frames and two hinged lenses. The two elasticated goggle straps are held against the back of the helmet by a leather loop (rear view opposite). The Type D oxygen mask with built-in microphone is fastened to the Type B, chamois-lined leather helmet by pressure studs. Earpieces fit inside zipped sockets on each side of the helmet. The regulation issue blue-grey woollen scarf is noteworthy.

of black
r and
canvas,
eepskin
n 40 flying
have
rubber
and
ieces. The
of the cuff
s by a

The reserve 'chute is hooked to two front harness buckles.

Below. **From top to bottom:**
Air Gunner wings: 1939 standard model.
Observer insignia: introduced in Britain in 1942, this Polish model was awarded to gunners and wireless operators. The manufacture's name 'J.R. Gaunt, Birmingham' is featured on the obverse side.
1944 Wireless Operator/Air Gunner wings.

CANADIAN INFANTRYMAN

Left.
Introduced in late 1943, the Mk III steel helmet was widely issued to the first Canadian troops ashore on D-Day. In the picture, the elasticated chinstrap is slipped over the brim. For improved camouflage, brown and green hessian strips have been worked into the netting. A field dressing was sometimes carried under the net.

The distinctive insignia sewn on the sleeves include the regimental and 'Canada' shoulder titles above the 3rd Division blue formation patch (the Canadians did not use the British 'arm of service strip' system).

The Canadian-manufactured battledress is darker and better made that the British 1937 Pattern model.

The Régiment de la Chaudière's cap badge refers to the unit's duty when raised in 1936: it was a machine gun regiment which was converted to the infantry role in 1941. The Latin motto means: 'Harder than iron'.

NORMANDY, 4 July 1944. Operation 'Windsor' is in full swing: the Canadians are involved in a bitter struggle to wrest the village of Carpiquet from the tough Panzergrenadiere of the 12th SS Division 'Hitlerjugend'.

Canadian-manufactured Lee Enfield N°4 Mk I*.

Left.
Identical to British personal equipment, Canadian kit can be differentiated by the yellower shade of the webbing (as typified by the bandoleer). The 'matchete' (bolo/combat knife) hangs from the belt in its dark brown leather sheath. The handle of the machete has two black Bakelite grips and a leather cord.

BY
Philippe
LAURENT
And
Bernard
PETITJEAN

ORMANDY, 1944

Right.
Rear view showing the canvas and leather braces (privately purchased ones were also used). The trousers only has one back pocket with a buttoned flap. The colour of the lining is typical. The beret is adjusted by means of a rayon cord, sliding through a green leather hem, and knotted at the back of the head. The markings of Canadian trousers were not indicated on a white cloth label but inked on the lining of one of the hip pockets.

In his large pack, the soldier carries spareboots, plimsolls, beret, rations, ammunition, mess kit and jumper. The rubberised ground sheet is folded under the pack flap (its reddish colour indicates its Canadian origin). The shovel is slipped into the large pack's straps and used in preference to the entrenching tool which was regarded as practically useless. The handle of the indispensable enamel mug dangles from one of the straps.

ight gasmask
rsack is slung
the shoulder;
de pockets
ain an anti-
ning outfit,
ective ointment
anti-gas
hields.

Blackened leather ankle boots with hobnailed soles.

Right.
With the exception of paras, armoured forces and Scottish traditional regiments, Canadian soldiers were issued with a khaki beret matching the colour of the uniform. The regimental cap badge is pinned onto the beret above the left eye. The trousers were an exact copy of the British 1937 Pattern: gathered around the ankles by a buttoned tab, they have a deep patch pocket with buttoned flap high up on the left leg. When worn without the blouse, the trousers are held up by a web waist belt slipped through the tabs (or a web trousers belt with plain prongless buckle). The collarless flannel shirt is identical to the British model but for its rather brownish shade and plastic buttons. The fibre ID tags hang from a thin cord.

THE 5TH (YORKSHIRE) DIVISION, 1940-1945

IN 1939 the 5th (Yorkshire) Regular Infantry Division was stationed in the county of Yorkshire. Its 13th and 15th Brigades were shipped to France in early October 1939 and reorganised into independent units.

In April 1940, the 5th Brigade was ferried to Norway and took part in the Narvik operation. After the May-June 1940 campaign, the 13th and 17th Brigades were repatriated for refitting.

In May 1942, the 13th and 17th Brigades landed in Madagascar to protect the island from the Japanese. This operation marked the end of a long and complicated journey that took the division from India, to Iraq and Persia when order in these countries was threatened by German agents. The division was then transferred to Syria and Egypt before taking part in the Sicily landings (9 July to 17 August 1943). On 9 September, the unit landed in Italy in the Reggio sector and was deployed in that theatre until the end of June 1944. On 3 July, the 5th Division was off to Egypt and Palestine and posted there from 9 July 1944 to 8 February 1945. The unit returned to Italy on 15 February before being ordered to Northern Europe.

Embarking in Naples in late February 1945, the Division landed at Marseilles on 1st March and was ferried by train to Ghent in Belgium. The unit was mustered in the region of Ulzen, in Germany, some 100km south of Hamburg. Consolidated within the 8th Corps, the Yorkshire Division took part in the Elbe crossings (Operation 'Enterprise') and contributed to the mopping up of the last pockets of German resistance. On 3 May, as the war was drawing to a close, the Division reached Lübeck on the Baltic Sea. No other British Army unit saw as much of the world in such a short time.

Left.

Holland, March 1945. Just arrived from Italy, this soldier from the 5th Division has been issued with new kit before going to the front. The combination of scarf, woollen gloves and leather jerkin convey the typical appearance of the British infantryman during the bitter 1944-45 winter campaign. The following insignia are displayed on the blouse sleeve: Northamptonshire Regiment title; the three strips of the 17th (third in order of precedence) Brigade; and traditional black regimental flash. The standard 1937 Pattern individual equipment includes two 1942 Pattern enlarged pouches for Sten magazines and with a green canvas haversack for the Light Respirator Mk I or II (slung over the left shoulder). The Mk II steel helmet is covered with camouflage netting and hessian strips. The soldier is armed with the N°4 Mk I* rifle.

THE MACHINE-GUN BATTALION

1-7th Battalion the Cheshire Regiment. S: The Order of the Garter appears on the cap badge. The oak leaves and the acorn were presented to the Regiment by King George II to celebrate their bravery during the battle of Dettingen. The badge is bi-metal but a plastic version also exists.

1-A: 5th Division formation sign. Printed model; the 'Y' stands for Yorkshire (a new insignia with a 'Y' on a black disc was introduced in 1946). The Division was commanded by Major-General R.A. Hull during the north-western European campaign.

Jean BOUCHERY

Left. Issued to foot soldiers in 1940, the greatcoat is made of a thick khaki woollen material. The double-breasted garment has shoulder tabs and two rows of three metal buttons down the front. The top of the coat is secured by two buttons and a brass hook sewn under the large lapels. While walking, the flaps of the skirt can be kept up by means of a hook and eyelet arrangement. At the back, a two-part half-belt is secured by three small buttons while a plaited slit sealing with two small buttons runs down the middle. Tan cotton lining is sewn at shoulder level and extends midway down the chest. The brass buttons are adorned with the British Royal coat of arms (royal crown over a standing lion and unicorn over the kingdom's emblems) with two mottos in French: 'Dieu et mon droit' and 'Honi soit qui mal y pense'. Some units have regimental buttons adorned with the regimental or branch of service insignia. Regulations specify that only the rank insignia and arm of service strip (scarlet here for line infantry) can be worn on the coat. The white cloth label sewn in the left flap of the skirt reads:

'Greatcoat, Dismounted 1940 Pattern Size N°4 height, Breast, G. Glenfield and sons, ⋀ 1942.

ow. Pattern 1940 Battledress trousers: made of different cloth, y can also be differentiated from the original 1937 Pattern by the k of button tabs at the waist, the visible button on the upper leg :ket and the large khaki flannel piece sewn on the inside for rmth. The General Service Cap was manufactured on British ectives by the Belgian firm Verschaffel of Gramont in 1945 with th provided by the RAOC. The size, measurements and War partment arrow are noteworthy. The British and American armies ced many orders with local manufacturers in the months owing the Liberation of Belgium.

Right.
Ghent, March 1945. The men of the 5th Infantry Division have been granted a few days' leave before returning to the front. This soldier of the 5th Essex enjoys a cuppa offered to him by the NAAFI. The man's serge general service cap sports the regimental Cap Badge on a purple backing. The cut of the thick greatcoat is well shown here. Awkward in action and quickly soaked in rainy conditions, this coat was disliked by the soldiers who found it better suited to garrison duties, leave or guard under shelter. In compliance with regulations, this private only wears the arm-of-service strips on each sleeve.

1941-1945
SOVIET FORCES

SOVIET SEAMAN 1940-45

By Pierre BESNAR

O N 25 December 1941 Soviet seamen were preparing for the amphibious assault of the Kerch peninsula where they fought as infantry. About 250 ships supported by more than 660 combat aircraft ferried the Russian forces to the opposite bank of the Kerch and to Feodosiya. Fighting went on until March 1942 when the Germans forced the Russians back towards the Caucasus.

'IN our country, the word "sailor" will forever be associated with supreme bravery, unshakeable determination, and unlimited dedication to military duty'.

Pravda, 1 March 1944.

Below.
Typical Red Navy items displayed on a navy flag:
1. Cap tallies. From top to bottom: Arctic Fleet; Baltic Fleet (with Order of the Red Flag award); Minesweeper (or minelayer) Brigade; tally awarded to units raised to 'Guards' status for exceptional bravery. The unit's name is printed on a ribbon in the Order of Glory colours. Officers and petty officers of the unit were awarded the Guards' metal badge.
2. Nakhimov Medal (created on 3 March 1944).
3. Ushakov Medal (created on 3 March 1944).
These two medal were only awarded to navy personnel.
Several Soviet Navy shoulder tabs (respectively white and dark blue for summer and winter uniforms).
4. Arctic Fleet ratings.
5. Petty Officer (Starshiy Krasnoflotets).
6. Arctic Fleet ratings (variant).
7. Baltic Fleet ratings.
A navy instruction manual provides the backdrop for a model 1942 minesweeper/minelayer (distinguished) specialist badge and a modified 1942 submarine commander badge.

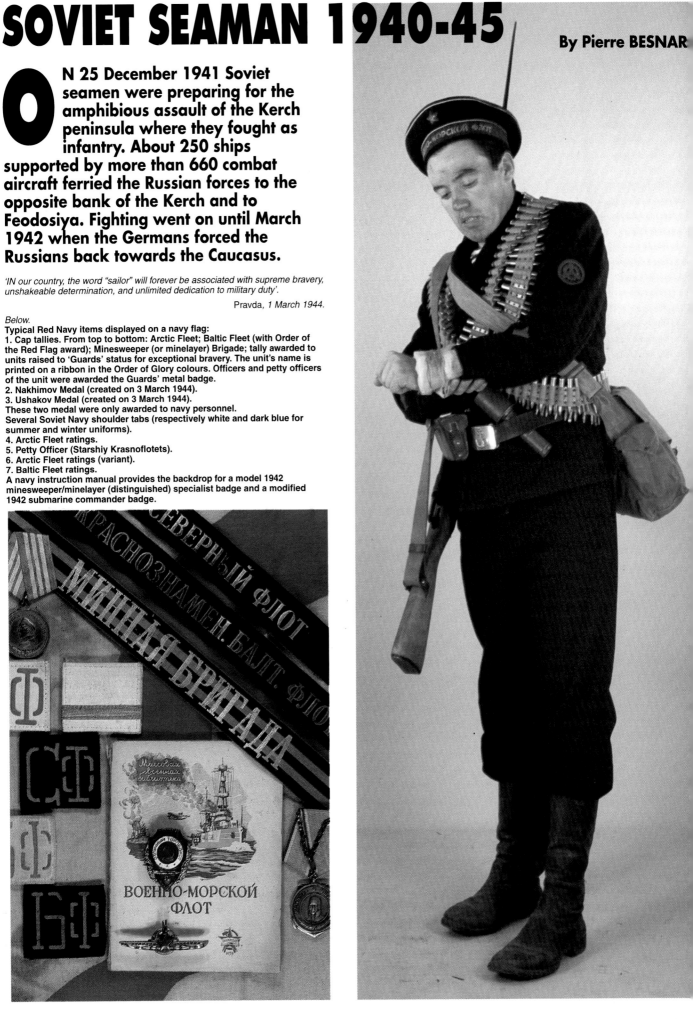

Spring 1940: During a trip to Sevastopol, the seaman has his photograph taken. He is seen in his Number One summer dress with white 'Flanelevka' seaman jumper, matching cap cover and black trousers. This outfit is worn from 1 May to 1 October. This uniform has hardly changed since the days of the Imperial Navy and is roughly identical to that of other nations' naval forces. Its most typical feature is the blue and white striped vest that can be worn with most outfits. Along with the vest, the cap's long ribbons are the Soviet sailor's most characteristic garments. Russian sailors used to go to great lengths to retain them in all circumstances. The man is pictured in front of the Soviet Navy's ensign.

Below. September 1943. The seaman has now been promoted to the rank of leading seaman (Starshiy Krasnoflotets) and is leading a recce party near Novorossisk before the counter-attack. His headgear is unchanged. The Order of the Red Star (right) and Defence of Sevastopol medals are prominently displayed on his dark blue 'Flanelevka' seaman's jumper (the Russians wore all their medals at all times). The Russian carries the ubiquitous canvas haversack and machine-gun ammunition belt wrapped around his body. He is armed with a PPSh 1941 submachine-gun fitted with a 35-round curved magazine. As a secondary weapon, he carries a TT 1933 pistol in a canvas holster.

Left. Sevastopol harbour, June 1944. A petty officer (Starshina Vtoroy Statii) takes a closer look at his trophy: a German dress dagger abandoned by a Kriegsmarine administration officer now on his long retreat towards the 'Vaterland'.The Russian still wears the 'Telogreika' padded jacket he was issued in the winter of 1943-44. Two 1930 Pattern vulcanised canvas cartridge pockets (wartime fabrication) are slipped on the belt. The cap, striped vest and gasmask haversack are also worn. A folder with a map of the Kerch area and binoculars supplement the equipment. The seaman is armed with a semi-automatic Tokarev rifle. A revolutionary weapon when introduced, the Tokarev proved too fragile and required careful maintenance. It was thus mostly issued to experienced NCOs and seamen. Its bayonet is suspended from the belt. The stencil on the ammunition crate reads 'mortar shells'.

The seaman (Krasnoflotets) whose rank insignia, a red star, appears on the sleeves, has donned ʀshlat' pea-jacket for the bitter 1941-42 campaign in which he sustained a wrist wound. The ⸱y reads 'Navy sailor'. The double-breasted serge pea-jacket has a double row of anchor-adorned ⸱s down the front. The specialist badge (mechanic) is sewn on the left shoulder. Fitted with a ⸱late, the leather belt carries a 1893 Imperial Pattern ammunition pouch and a 1933 Pattern ⸱renade. The BN gasmask is carried in a haversack slung over the left hip. Due to the shortage ⸱rsacks in the Red Army, the sailor may well have discarded his gasmask and replaced it with ⸱al items or food!Characteristically, Soviet sailors carried spare machine-gun ammunition in ⸱as here, a belt for a PM 1910 machine-gun. This practice considerably increased the ammunition ⸱of Russian machine-gunners (theoretically, each infantry battalion had 15 machine-guns). The ⸱a 1891/30 Mosin Nagant with bayonet. The boots are standard army issue.

SOVIET PARA, 1935-45

By Gérard GOROKHOFF

OPERATIONAL at the outbreak of World War 2, Soviet airborne forces disappeared during the German advance or were wasted in bloody battles of attrition during 1943. Soviet paratroopers often fought successfully alongside partisans but never in the role for which they had been trained.

Left.
'Desantnik', 1941-43
Only the 'Gymnastiorka' early type collar tabs indicate air force personnel. The side cap and PPSh-41 submachine-gun are standard infantry issue (in those days, there weren't such things as folding butts or sophisticated jump helmets!). The Soviet para's most typical outfit is the green and brown two-piece oversuit with typical cloud shaped camouflage pattern. In this picture, the blouse has faded more with age than the trousers. Like the trousers, the blouse is fastened around the waist with a drawstring and has two access slits. The legs are tightened by tapes at the hem, and slippedinside the boots.

Above.
Fastened by three cupped buttons, the hood has a muslin faceveil and is wide enough to be worn over a helmet or fur hat.

Left.
Airborne officer wearing the 1939-45 service dress. Introduced in 1943, the 'Kittel' tunic has two chest pockets and a standing collar with cornflower blue piping (the Air Force branch of service colour) repeated on the shoulder tabs, the turn-back cuffs and the mid-blue trousers. The airborne qualification badge is pinned above the left chest pocket where it was worn until the end of the war. The air force insignia -wings with an embroidered cockade - appears on the khaki peaked cap with blue band and piping. The gilt braid shoulder tabs may be worn with the service and the parade dresses. They are adorned with the Air Force gilt insignia and a star indicating the rank of second lieutenant.

Below.
Rank badges and airborne wings (issued until 1943)
A. NCO 'triangle'.
B. Subaltern 'square'.
C. Field rank officer 'rectangle'.
NB: A, B, and C insignia are worn on the collar tabs.
D. Early issue wings.
E. Early issue wings variant.
F. Shoulder and collar tab air force insignia.
G. 1935 1st Class instructor badge.
H. 2nd Class instructor badge.
I. 3rd Class instructor badge.
J. 1938 instructor badge, which replaced the 1935 Pattern but was often worn alongside it.

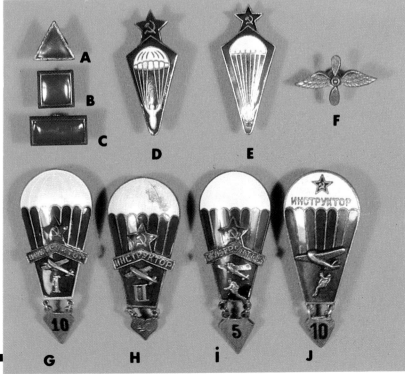

SOVIET TANK BUSTER, 1942-1943

Jan RUTKIEWICZ
Pictures : Lech ALEXANDROWICZ

IN the winter of 1941-42, Russian infantrymen were issued with more potent weapons to tackle Nazi armour and as a consequence, German tanks soon began to fall prey to PTRD-41 and PTRS-41 anti-tank rifles.

Stalingrad barred the way to the Wehrmacht's armoured divisions. Whoever held that city conrolled the routes into southern Russia, the road network and even more important, the traffic on the Volga.

'*Not one step back!*' ordered Stalin. '*The invaders must be checked in front of Stalingrad like they were in front of Moscow!*'

The Russians implemented all the measures they felt were necessary to boost the Red Army, distributing leaflets extolling Soviet patriotism and raising to Guards status the bravest units. To prevent subversion, every soldier or civilian suspected of sabotage, espionage or defeatism was immediatley put to death by NKVD flying squads.

1943: Equipped with the 1940 Pattern steel helmet, this tank buster wears the 1943 Pattern tunic with straight collar and two buttons. His rank (sergeant) is indicated by the three red stripes on the 1943 Pattern shoulder tabs. The 1935 Pattern khaki serge trousers have matching knee insets. The blue-grey cotton puttees are worn with brown leather hobnailed boots. The leather reinforced web belt is a wartime production. The gas mask is carried in a sturdy canvas haversack; the standard issue entrenching tool is slipped into the belt, and the weapon is a PTRD-41 anti-tank rifle

1942-43: The man wears a 1936 Pattern helmet and 1935 Pattern khaki serge tunic with turn down collar. Collar tabs for the combat uniform were introduced in August 1941 and sport enamelled rank insignia (the two triangles indicate a sergeant). The two chest pockets have flaps fastened by embossed metal buttons adorned with a star. The new rank insignia were reintroduced along with the collar tabs in early 1943. The 1938 gallantry medal and the Guards enamelled insignia are pinned on the chest. The weapon is a PTRD-41.

Soviet Union: an NKVD political commissar in the summer of 1941. The 'Politrouk' (Politicheskiy Roukovoditiel) wears the 1935 pattern cap with ersatz material peak and black chinstrap. The peaked cap is in blue service colours with red piping. The 1935 Pattern 'Gymnastiorka' with fall collar has two chest pockets closing with star adorned buttons. The collar and ornaments are dark pink. The ranker's collar tabs (in the service colour) are plain (gilt braid or service insignia were issued only to officers). The two red enamelled pips indicate the rank of 'Mladishiy Politrouk' a rank equivalent to second-lieutenant. The gilt stars with red piping on the sleeves were the hallmark of political commissars.

The 1930 Order of the Red Star (probably awarded during the 1939 Polish campaign or in Finland) and the NKVD distinguished service insignia are pinned to the chest. The brown leather 1932 Pattern belt with cross strap has a two-pronged buckle and carries a holster for a Nagan pistol. A Pattern 1935 belt with brass plate (featuring a cut-out star) was also seen.

The 1932 Pattern corduroy trousers are dark blue with dark pink piping. They are gathered into standard officers high boots. The 'Harmochka' (accordion) patterned boots present the typical cuff deformation.

By Jan RUTKIEWICZ
pictures: Lech ALEXANDROWICZ

I still remember the scorching summer of 1944, somewhere in eastern Poland. Operation 'Bagration' was in full swing. The last members of a Latvian SS Division proved no match for the overwhelming power of the Red Army. The liberators were coming... Broken with fatigue, good-natured Soviet 'frontoviks' comforted us: *'Don't be afraid of us soldiers, but rather fear instead those who follow, the NKVD troops!'*

NKVD UNIFORMS, 1917-45

A: 1922 Pattern. Left: a GPU soldier with typical dark green collar tabs, red piping and green ornamental buttoned tabs. The green cap star is also piped in red. Right: A 'Komandir' from the KSR (KGB troops protecting the Republic's supply convoys). His blue collar tabs are piped in red; the coat has blue ornamental buttoned chest tabs. The rank badge on the left sleeve (two squares and a red star) features the distinctive red piping.

B: 1924-25 Pattern: Left KSR officer in 'French khaki' with red shoulder tabs piped in dark red. Dark grey trousers with dark red piping. The blue cap has a red crown with red piping. Right, a ranker wearing a dark grey Boudiennovka balaklava helmet. The dark red collar tabs are also piped in dark red.

(From 'Your Uniform in War', illustrated by VN Koulikov, Ministry of the Interior, Moscow, 1896).

NKVD border guard, USSR, 1939-40. This ranker's 1935 Pattern cap has the typical green and dark blue service colours. The representative green collar tabs of his 1935 Pattern greatcoat (Shinel) are piped in red; rankers' boots were made of black ersatz leather. The brown leather belt holds a sturdy canvas ammunition pouch (one of several types on issue). The guard is armed with a Pattern 1890-30 7.62mm Mosin rifle fitted with its bayonet *(Shtik)*.

NKVD SERVICE COLOURS

JANUARY 1922 REGULATIONS

GPU collar tab and headgear star

KSR collar tabs and headgear star

1924-25 AMENDMENTS

1935 REGULATIONS

Officer-general's collar tab

Officer' collar tab

Collar tab issued to rank and file and administrative staff

Left.
NKVD infantryman, Soviet Union, 1939-40. The 1935 Pattern soft cap has the NKVD blue and red service colours. The 1935 Pattern 'Gymnastiorka' is made of khaki coloured cotton and adorned with dark red collar tabs piped in dark pink sporting the service's metal insignia (target and crossed rifles). The 'Komsomol' (communist youth) insignia is pinned to the right side of the chest. The regulation issue trousers have reinforcements at the knees. The boots are made of ersatz leather. The dark brown regular issue belt carries the canvas ammunition pouches for the Model 1891/30 Mosin rifle with socket bayonet.

Right.
An NKVD 'Srarshiy Leytnant' (lieutenant), somewhere in the USSR, winter 1941-42. This officer in service dress wears the 1935 Pattern blue peaked cap with dark pink and dark red piping. The double-breasted greatcoat's (Shinel) collar is adorned with dark red tabs and gold braid. The three red square symbols and the service insignia indicate the rank of NKVD line lieutenant (like the three stripes on the sleeve). A 1932 Pattern Sam Browne belt and boots complete the equipment.

ove.
tumn 1941: NKVD troops on their way to the front. The
llar tabs, the rank insignia and the branch of service
dge (target and crossed rifles) are noteworthy.

Left.
Soviet memorabilia displayed on one of the leaflets the Luftwaffe dropped by the trousands to urge Russian troops to surrender: a Pattern 1895 Nagant handgun with its 7.62mm ammunition (the bullets are carried in the holster); a 1938 three-rouble banknote, an NKVD captain's gold badge; a political commissar's red star (piped in gold, these stars were worn instead of and in place of the rank badges issued to line officers) and the NKVD Distinguished Service Insignia.

NKVD major (Mayor) in the Soviet Union, 1943-44, with 1935 Pattern field cap piped in the service colour. The 1943 Pattern tunic (Kitel) with standing collar seals and five star adorned gilt buttons. The collar and adornments are piped in light blue which became the NKVD's service colour in 1943. This colour is repeated on the shoulder tabs with rank insignia (a star). The 1933 Tokarev pistol is carried in a leather holster suspended from a belt worn under the tunic. The numerous medals and orders displayed on the chest include:
Left:
- 1924 Order of the Red Star.
- 1943 First class Order of Glory.
- 1938 'For Valor' medal.
Right:
- 1930 Order of the Red Star.
- 1942 Order of the Great Patriotic War.
- NKVD Distinguished Service Order.
1942 Guards insignia (several NKVD units were raised to this status). The 1932 Pattern officers' breeches are made of dark blue serge and piped in light blue in accordance with 1943 regulations.

PARADE DRESS

Above.
An excerpt from the 1935 regulation handbook. Left an NKVD officer in raglan trench coat with officers' dark red collar tabs (dark pink piping), silver braid and triangular rank insignia. The man is a subaltern officer as the three red triangles on the lower sleeve indicate.

Right: a ranker in 'Gymnastiorka' (blouse); red collar tabs piped in dark pink and trooper's blue braid. The service insignia is pinned at the rear end of the collar tab.

(From Your Uniform in War, *illustrated by VN Koulikov, Ministry of the Interior, Moscow, 1896).*

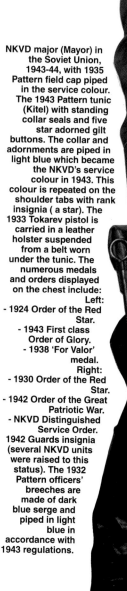

Right.
An NKVD colonel (Polkovnik) somewhere in eastern Europe in 1943-44. The man is clad in a winter service dress topped off with a 1943 Pattern grey astrakhan 'Papachka'. The headgear has a grey crown with cross gold braid. Unlike the 'Papachkha' exclusively worn by generals, marshals and colonels, the star was issued to all ranks. The 1943 Pattern double breasted dress coat is light grey and has a double row of star adorned gilt buttons down the front. In compliance with 1943 regulations, the dark blue shoulder tabs of the NKVD officers' service dress are piped in light blue.

...ve.
...ldier in grey serge 'Shinel' with a 'Papachkha' head dress. ...ar tabs are dark red with blue piping. Gilt buttons. The ...er in walking-out dress wears the cap adorned with the ...ice colours. The collar tabs and ornaments of his 'Kitel' ...dark blue like the breeches.

1943 PATTERN NKVD UNIFORMS

Like the Red Army's, NKVD uniforms were thoroughly updated in 1943.

Rank and File Insignia

Field uniform shoulder tabs are khaki with dark red piping. Plain rank braid with Burgundy wine piping. Dress uniform shoulder tabs are dark blue with red piping. Unit emblems, figures and letters are painted on (for example: 156K 156 'Konvoi' Battalion). The Shinel collar tabs are dark red with blue piping (dress uniform) and khaki with dark red piping (field uniform).

Officers' Insignia

The shoulder tabs of officers' field and service dresses were piped in blue. The coat (dress and field) shoulder tabs had respectively a blue and a khaki backing with light blue piping.

The piping of the 'Kitel' is dark blue like the breeches.

Left.
Officer in field dress, 1943. Cap with distinctive colours, khaki 'Gymnastiorka' with Sam Browne belt, gold and blue shoulder tabs, khaki breeches and black leather high boots.

1941-1945
AMERICAN FORCES

US INFANTRY EQUIPMENT 1941-42

By Philippe Charbonnier

ON Monday 22 December 1941 at 2am, 43,000 Japanese soldiers led by Lieutenant General Homma (Japanese XIV Army) stormed the shore of the Lingayen Gulf, some 150km west of Manila. Just a fortnight after the attack on Pearl Harbor, the fall of Guam and the assault on Wake, the American bastion in the Philippines was next to be engulfed by the Japanese tidal wave.

This close-up is devoted to the American infantryman of that era. As the months went by, the American soldier's typical appearance quickly evolved into the familiar silhouette of the victorious GI.

In 1941, the uniforms issued to American troops by the Quartermaster Corps were still strongly reminiscent of those worn in 1918. Prewar modernisation efforts were mostly devoted to a long and tedious exchange of proposals between the services, sometimes followed by experiments by specialised commissions. In autumn 1939, when President Roosevelt felt that America could be drawn into the war, none of the modernisation projects had borne fruit. It was around that time that improved, more functional uniforms were designed for American servicemen.

Opposite, left.
April 1942: an infantryman from 31st Infantry Regiment, on duty on the Bataan Peninsula in the Philippines. The man is clad in summer uniform.

Page 85, from left to right.
An infantryman from the 34th Infantry Division, in Northern Ireland, autumn 1942. The winter uniform with overcoat was worn while disembarking in Northern Ireland but was used mostly on parades or off duty.

The soldier depicted here is a survivor from his regiment, the only American unit consolidated within Filipino forces. This regiment was practically annihilated during the campaign. The combat uniform is the standard summer service dress.

Devoid of any insignia, the khaki cotton shirt has faded in the sun.

Introduced in the Great War, t[he] M-1917 A1 steel helmet was modified in 1937 through the addition of a quick release ch[in] strap and an improved leather lining.

The canvas bandolier contains twelve .30. cartridge clips. Th[e] length of its strap adjusted by mea[ns] a safety pin.

Springfield M-1903 A1 rifle fitted with a leather sling and an M-1907 bayonet. The semi-automatic Garand was on standard issue by then, although most soldiers in this theatre were still armed with the time tested '03'.

The Pattern 19[10] web cartridge [belt] was on regular issue to infantry along with the canteen and field dressing pocket. M-1910 bayonet scabbard was wor[n on] the left.

Short of anything better, the traini[ng] gas mask was widely distribut[ed]. It was carried i[n a] long pouch slu[ng] over the should[er] and secured by [a] cord at the waist.

The 1938 Pattern gaiters were on regular issue to foot soldiers. Made of canvas, they were issued in 1939 for field service.

Prewar standard service shoes were of chromed leather, had toecaps, rubber heels and leather soles. They had the same russet colour as other American leather equipment.

Made of light tan cotton, the straight trousers have five pockets: one on ea[ch] side, one on each h[ip] and a fob pocket at [the] front. The web belt [had] a black metal, prongless buckle. T[he] World War 1 Pattern breeches were repla[ced] with straight trousers [in] January 1938. Desig[ned] for garrison duties, t[he] trousers often prove[d] too close fitting for combat.

ned in the prewar years, the
on cap was first issued to
rps and armoured forces
nnel (the campaign hat was
y suited to their duties). On
re of the conflict, a new
gear known as Field or
eas Cap was designed and
d to all services. Cut in
wool (or light tan for wear
the summer service dress),
ip was piped around the
n in the branch-of-service
r. The distinctive insignia
inned to the front.
use of its
ess design,
ip was not
ed to
ine duties
oon
ne known
garrison

Overcoat: worn here over the
wool service coat, it was
made of thick woollen cloth
and patterned as per 1940
regulations. The garment
has a double row of
buttons down the front,
shoulder tabs, a buttoned
half-belt as well as two
large back darts. Originally
designed for winter duty,
the coat
proved too

This soldier is
shown in full kit.
American
soldiers
garrisoned in the
UK held fequent
parades to get better
acquainted with
British forces and
population.

The M-1917 A1 steel
helmet was soon
replaced by the new
M-1 issued in 1941.

Individual equipment
included items introduced
in peacetime: M-1928
haversack, M-1923 cartridge
belt, M-1924 field dressing
pocket, and M-1910
canteen. Fastened to the
left-hand side of the
haversack, the bayonet
is carried in a
plastic scabbard
introduced in
April 1942.

r's
s are
cted by
n woollen
s.

shoes
shoes,
) were
over the
e shoes
d or
weather
tions.
odel
n here is
ewar all-
r type.

Introduced
in 1938 the
woollen serge
trousers
superseded the
breeches (made of
the same cloth). The
pattern was that of
the summer trousers.

M-1938 leggings
on issue to
dismounted
troops.

The
M 1939
service coat.
Open collar service
coats were
introduced in 1926
and fulfilled a dual
dress/combat
purpose until
replaced by the M-
1941 field jacket. The
model shown here
became standard
issue in 1939. It has
two pleats in the back
and two hooks for the
leather garrison belt
worn with service
dress. The front is
done up with four gilt
buttons. The jacket
has two chest patch
pockets and two
bellowed inner
pockets on the hips.
The rectangular flaps
bear the same buttons
as the shoulder tabs.
The only insignia
displayed on the
jacket are the collar
discs.

f the two sturdy
n 'barracks' bags
d to every
emen. The 'A'
capital letter
ting the
nts were
lled on
ont

ic
ng

US RANGERS, DIEPPE, 1942

WHEN the United States declared war on Germany in 1942, President Roosevelt requested that small commando units be raised. That summer, American Colonel Lucian K. Truscott went to Britain and arranged that American soldiers would take part in any raids the British carried out in occupied Europe.

By Philippe CHARBONNIER

Left. this Ranger belongs to the 40-man detachment attached to N°3 Commando. Most of these soldiers, however, were to play no part in the action. In true commando fashion, the man has blackened his face. The Pattern 1942 herringbone twill overall has two patch pockets (chest and back), two buttoned hip pockets and ankle tabs. The M-1917A1 helmet is covered with British netting. No leggings are worn. A grey undershirt (as here) or a flannel shirt could be worn under the overall. As a machine-gunner, the soldier has been issued with a M1911A1 pistol he carries in an M-1916 leather holster hooked onto the eyelets of his M-1936 web belt. Slipped on the belt, an M-1912 magazine pocket contains spare ammunition for the pistol. The belt is held by the braces of the M-1928 haversack used here without its lower part (pack carrier). (Coleman Collection).

Right. One of four Americans with N°4 Commando, this Ranger is clad in a mixture of early American kit and British equipment. For easier identification, the man wears a British woolknit cap comforter. The standard combat uniform includes: flannel shirt (early model with front placket), serge trousers with vertical slit pockets; 1938 Pattern leggings with brass hooks and early russet leather service shoes with toecaps. Rifle ammunition is carried in the M-1923 cartridge belt and in the cotton bandoleers crossed on the chest. As a team leader, the man has M-1938 wirecutters suspended from his belt. The M-1928 haversack mess kit pouch is tied to the belt; it contains Mills bombs. Bren gun magazines and more hand grenades are carried in the British regulation small pack slung over the shoulder. The M-1 rifle is fitted with a 1907 Pattern sling. (Coleman Collection).

US RANGERS, 4th BATTALION, ANZIO, 1944

ON 22 January 1944, General John P. Lucas' 6th Corps landed at Anzio and pushed seven miles inland. The amphibious assault, however, soon turned into a stalemate reminiscent of World War 1 trench warfare: the beachhead was kept under continuous German fire while the Luftwaffe disrupted Allied supply and reinforcement efforts.

By Philippe CHARBONNIER

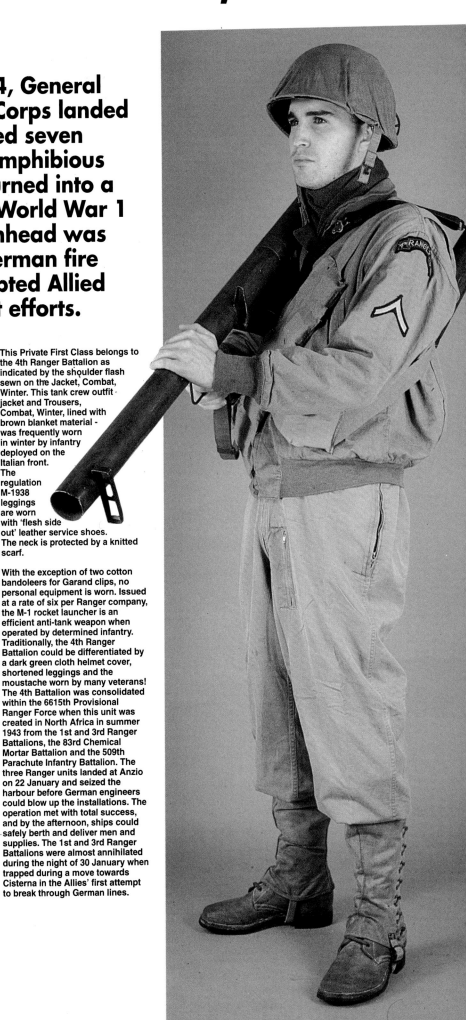

Below. February 1944: getting supply trucks through Anzio's devastated streets has become a matter of life or death for the Allies. The bombing has been severe as evidenced by the wrecked buildings in the background. The obscure but vital task of directing traffic has been entrusted to British and American military police. To speed up the delivery of supplies, trucks were loaded onto LST's in Naples from where they sailed to Anzio to unload their cargo. At left, Lance Corporal Stedman wears an MP armband with red lettering on a blue background. His individual equipment has been blancoed. At right, Private Flynn of 5th Army wears a variant of the standard MP armband over the left sleeve of his M-1941 jacket (the armband is secured with elasticated straps). The letters 'MP' appear on the front of the helmet. Flynn is armed with an USM1 carbine. The tactical sign on the Chevrolet of Canada truck in the background (a '68' figure painted in white on a brown background) indicates that the vehicle belongs to the 2nd battalion, 3rd brigade of a British infantry division. (IWM)

This Private First Class belongs to the 4th Ranger Battalion as indicated by the shoulder flash sewn on the Jacket, Combat, Winter. This tank crew outfit - jacket and Trousers, Combat, Winter, lined with brown blanket material - was frequently worn in winter by infantry deployed on the Italian front. The regulation M-1938 leggings are worn with 'flesh side out' leather service shoes. The neck is protected by a knitted scarf.

With the exception of two cotton bandoleers for Garand clips, no personal equipment is worn. Issued at a rate of six per Ranger company, the M-1 rocket launcher is an efficient anti-tank weapon when operated by determined infantry. Traditionally, the 4th Ranger Battalion could be differentiated by a dark green cloth helmet cover, shortened leggings and the moustache worn by many veterans! The 4th Battalion was consolidated within the 6615th Provisional Ranger Force when this unit was created in North Africa in summer 1943 from the 1st and 3rd Ranger Battalions, the 83rd Chemical Mortar Battalion and the 509th Parachute Infantry Battalion. The three Ranger units landed at Anzio on 22 January and seized the harbour before German engineers could blow up the installations. The operation met with total success, and by the afternoon, ships could safely berth and deliver men and supplies. The 1st and 3rd Ranger Battalions were almost annihilated during the night of 30 January when trapped during a move towards Cisterna in the Allies' first attempt to break through German lines.

US FORCES, ANZIO, MAY 1944

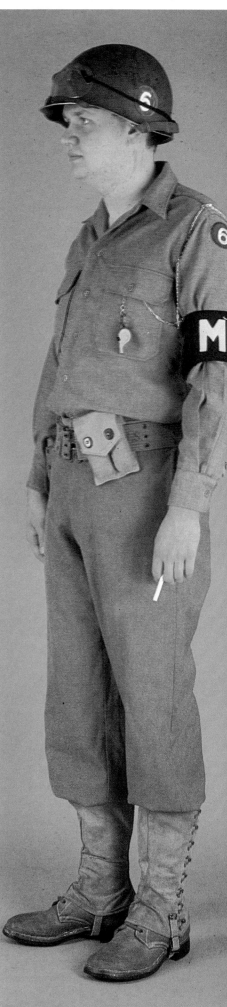

Right.
After the Allied breakthrough, Anzio harbour continued to be used to supply the troops sweeping up towards Rome. This Military Policeman from 6th Corps supervises traffic at an important crossroad. The 6th Corps insignia appears on the left sleeve of the standard issue shirt and is repeated on the helmet. Anti-gas eyeshields protect his eyes from dust. Indispensible to any policeman, the brass whistle dangles from a privately purchased chain. The armband is fastened with safety pins. The trousers are standard issue as are the gaiters and 'flesh out' leather service shoes. The M1911A1 pistol in its M-1916 russet leather hoslter is suspended from the M-1936 belt. The M-1916 web ammunition pouch is of World War 1 vintage.

Left.
This American officer from the 45th Infantry Division is an artillery observer who works with the infantry in the front line. He is issued with field glasses and a compass (carried in a special pocket hanging from the belt). Usually, artillery observers were accompanied by a radio operator equipped with a SCR-300 set. This second lieutenant is pictured in Anzio at the end of May when the weather was improving, as shown by the open collar of his officer's shirt. This is the dark olive drab combat type with shoulder tabs. The divisional patch appears on the left shoulder. Metal insignia, the crossed guns of field artillery and the gilt rank bar are respectively pinned to the left and right lapels. His helmet is covered with a piece of camouflage parachute cloth. Issued to enlisted men but often worn in combat by officers, the regulation serge trousers are held by a web belt with an officer-type brass buckle. The trouser legs are gathered into paratroopers' jumpboots presumably purloined by the soldier who found them more comfortable. Officers were usually armed with US M-1 carbines supplemented by a M1911A1 handgun carried in a holster. Pistol ammunition is carried in a 1923 Pattern web pocket, and carbine magazines in the double pocket slipped on the weapon's butt.

Around that time, some front line troops were issued with HBT fatigue uniforms which were better suited for the warmer climate but quickly abandoned on advice from officers who felt that their peculiar colour led to confusion with the German 'feldgrau'.

Page 90, bottom
1 February 1944: reinforcements are reaching the 36th Engineer Combat Regiment. In the picture, a Private first class assists a comrade who has just alighted from the LST in the background. The canvas 'barracks bag' (early type) was still on regular issue during the Anzio operation. Devoid of any carrying handles or straps, this bag was awkward to carry and consequently unpopular with the troops. Interestingly, some of the men have not yet been issued with regulation gaiters. The man on the left wears a tank crewman's overall on top of his trousers. The PFC's 'tanker's jacket' is of the early type as evidenced by the patch pockets on the chest. The unit insignia is visible on the upper sleeve.
(National Archives).

US ENGINEER, ANZIO, 1944

THE 36th Combat Engineer Regiment was raised in June 1941. The unit left the United States in November 1942 to take part in Operation 'Torch', the codename given to the Allied landings in North Africa.

The regiment served in Sicily and Salerno and was deployed during amphibious Operation 'Shingle' at Anzio in January 1944.

'H' Company landed with the Rangers in Anzio harbour to set up beacons on the shore and clear ordnance. The remainder of the regiment disembarked later and set about clearing the debris caused by the bombings. Meanwhile, special groups retrieved the explosive charges the Germans had placed in the harbour which, fortunately, they had no time to detonate before withdrawing. The engineers completed their mission on the beachhead by fighting as infantry, manning defensive positions and relieving various British and American units

Left.
Faithfully reconstructed from a contemporary photograph, this engineer is seen with a US M-1 helmet (without camouflage netting). On standard issue to tank crews, the winter combat jacket has a brown blanket lining and closes with a front zipper. The garment has knitted collar and cuffs, and was highly sought after by soldiers who went to any lengths to obtain one, especially after the M-1941 jacket had shown its shortcomings in North Africa. The unit patch is sewn on the left shoulder. The woollen trousers are tucked into light white woollen socks. Made o f 'rough side out' leather, the 1943 service shoes have no toecaps. The man is armed with a M-1903 Springfield rifle fitted with an M-1907 sling. Ammunition is carried in an M-1923 cartridge belt. The leather pouch containing pliers and an electrician's knife - quite handy for engineers' work - was obtained from signallers. The equipment is worn with M-1936 web suspenders.
The M-1926 Navy lifebelt is worn around the waist as was compulsory during crossings. The heavy gasmask (weighing 2.5kg) is visible under the left arm. This item is carried in a Mk IV canvas haversack slung over the shoulder and tied to the waist by adjustable quick-release straps.

1943-44 NEW US AMERICAN COMBAT UNIFORM

1943-1944, LES NOUVEAUX HABITS DE L'ARMÉE AMÉRICAINE

Worn for the first time in action on the 1943 Anzio beachhead, the M-1943 equipment marked a breakthrough in the design of military clothing. Research conducted by the Quartermaster Corps at the outbreak of the war led the Americans to differentiate between combat and service dresses and to design their field equipment accordingly.

The range of combat clothing evolved for use in the field also catered for the specific needs of the new service arms such as airborne, armoured, mountain troops etc.

Initial studies made in 1940-42 indicated that serious problems would result from the manufacture, storage and distribution of such a wide range of specialised items - some of which were meant for the same purpose. During the 1942-43 phase of studies, the Quartermaster Corps decided that all the specific items ought to be compatible with a standard uniform which would be issued to all the services. Consequently in autumn 1942, the idea of a standard combat outfit was put forward and samples were made.

Made of windproof and sturdy 'sateen' cotton, the two-piece dress was suitable for wear as an all-weather uniform in temperate climates. The ddition of a synthetic pile liner reputedly made it proof against the most extreme weather conditions. This combination led to several garments being phased out: the Mackinaw coat, the 'Melton' overcoat, the olive drab field jacket as well as special clothing.

The M-1943 Field Uniform (February 1943)

Tested by the Quartermaster Corps in summer 1943, the M-1943 range included a whole series of new clothing and equipment:
- M-1943 jacket and trousers (with braces), both items compatible with synthetic liners.
  - Combat boots ('buckle boots')
  - Wool/cotton socks reinforced at wear points.
  - Green canvas jungle P (pack).
  - Woollen hooded sleeping bag and waterproof case.
  - Waterproof poncho/shelter half.
  - Collapsible canteen.
  - Sweater with buttoned collar.
  - M-1936 pistol belt with pouches compatible with M-1 Garand and M-1 carbine ammo clips.
  - Ski cap.

In its conclusions, the Quartermaster Corps objected to the whole M-1943 set being retained but suggested that some of its components be issued. The combat jacket entered the US Army's inventory in December 1943.

Below. **On 10 April 1944, members of the 3rd Infantry Division are testing the new M-1943 combat dress. The jackets and trousers seen on soldiers Grillo and De Villa are made of cotton sateen, the first type of cloth used for the manufacture of garments. The shade of olive drab is quite dark. Buttoning at shoulder level, the hood meant for wear with the jacket is worn by the soldier on the right. The helmet net was also on recent issue; made of woven material, it was secured by a neoprene band. The M-1943 cap (inspired by the ski cap) appears to be worn under the steel helmet's liner. The man on the left is trying on comfort garments: a large scarf of worsted wool and a sweater with high, buttoned collar.** *(National Archives)*

Above.
May 1944: A GI of 3rd US ID at the rear during a lull. The man has just returned from QMC distribution point after being issued with new equipment.
The unit's distinctive insignia has been painted on the helmet liner. He wears a sweater with buttoned collar over his shirt. His M-1943 trousers have already been washed several times and show traces of wear. His leather and rubber 'shoe pacs' were already being tested in Italy during that period being worn with several pairs of thick woollen socks. Because of his poor eyesight, the man has been issued with regulation glasses. He carries a set of 'K' rations in addition to a wool sleeping bag carried in its green cotton waterproof case.

US COAST GUARD

By Pierre Besnard

Wearing the summer dress cap with light tan crown, the US Coast Guards' Lieutenant Commander is about to blow his whistle to direct a manoeuvre. The whistle and the torch slipped in the pocket of the lined trousers are the most representative tools of his trade. His function is also indicated by the armband on the left arm.

M1 steel helmet repainted 'Battleship Grey' by the navy.

Attached to the 1st Special Engineer brigade, this Beachmaster answers to the Naval Beach Battalions set up by the US Navy for 'Overlord', the landings in Normandy in June 1944. He is on duty in the 'Easy' sector of Omaha Beach, regulating traffic to the beachhead and supervising the unloading of the landing craft.

US Navy windproof poplin jacket. Identical to the US Army khaki drill M 1941 model, it can be differentiated by its colour and lack of shoulder tabs and cuff straps. The garment seals with a concealed front zipper. A black US Navy marking is stamped on the left front.

Sitting on a crate, the officer is trying to work out where to store the quantities of supplies delivered by the landing craft. His 6 x 3 M3 binoculars and BC611 walkie talkie are precious auxiliaries to manage the traffic. The bullion cap badge replaces the metal model often seen. The standard issue US Navy officers' cap sports the Coast Guards insignia.

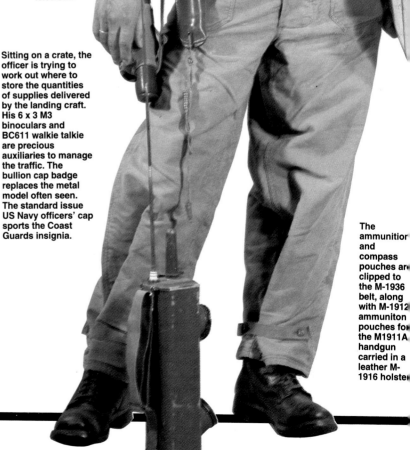

The ammunition and compass pouches are clipped to the M-1936 belt, along with M-1912 ammuniton pouches for the M1911A handgun carried in a leather M-1916 holster

EACHMASTER, 1944

The black tie is not lipped betwwen the ond and third collar button, a practice reserved to 'foot sloggers'.

The captain is bout to fire a flare to signal off a wave of awaitig landing barges. He has donned his steel helmet and sunglasses. The Navy issue shirt has no shoulder tabs (even for officers) while the rank insignia pinned to the lapels (gilt oakleaves) are smaller than Army models. These insignia indicate that the officer is sea command qualified.

USM1 carbine with ammunition pouches fastened to the butt. Aluminium canteen and M-1910 canvas haversack.

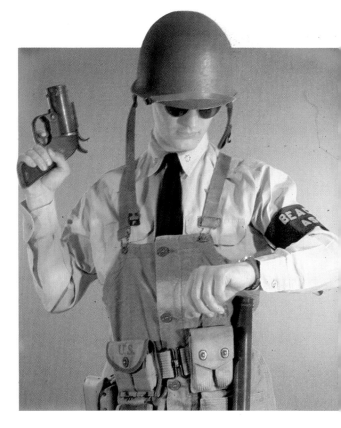

US Coast Guards' paraphernalia displayed on a Normandy ordnace chart. From top to bottom: a USM-1 steel helmet with painted rank insignia (lieutenant) and Coast Guard badge next to a liner in its typical 'Battleship Grey' livery. Signalling equipment: a torch and an AN M8 40mm flare pistol. A warrant officer's garrison cap insignia (pinned to the left side), a warant officer 2nd Class insignia (pinned to the right side) and lieutenant rank insignia. Below: a commander dark blue garrison cap under a summer model with Coast Guards officer insignia. Bottom from left to right: lieutenant junior grade shoulder tabs; ensign, Lieutenant and Lieutenant Commander (respectively dark blue serge and light grey cotton for dress uniform and fatigues). The ID tags of a Coast Guards Reserve member are displayed on an astronomical chart. Botom right, the USCG's armband.

e M-4 smask ried in an M6 ersack slung er the ulder. model more widely buted Navy onnel beach duties an the smask ued to ssault ps or navy onnel.

US Navy lined dungarees with back patch pockets and ankle straps.

Standard issue ankle boots. A Navy model in rough leather was also worn. Markings are indicated inside the cuff.

US ENGINEER OFFICE[R]

By Jacques ALLUCHON

THE 6,000 men of 10 Engineer Combat Battalions were among the first troops ashore at dawn on D-Day. Theirs was no easy task: to blast the way open for the 60,000 infantrymen who followed.

Left. This heavily laden lieutenant hints at the particular nature of the mission with his specialised equipment. In addition to individual equipment, the engineers carried demolition materiel in the assault vest widely issued to first wave troops. This officer carries the same kit as his men and can only be differentiated by his M-1 carbine, pistol and helmet rank insignia (a white vertical bar). Specially designed for amphibious operations, the M-5 gasmask in its rubberised haversack is slung around the neck. However, as the gasmask got in the way of the vest chest pockets, it was probably discarded after the first beach obstacles had been overcome.

As a necessa[ry] precaution on this chil[l] June morning, the offic[er] has donned a woolle[n] shirt under his fie[ld] jacket.The gas mas[k] haversack and the M-[2] life preserver are fastene[d] on the chest over the ves[t] while the M-1936 web be[lt] supporting the M1911[A] pistol and M-193[?] wirecutters is worn und[er] the garme[nt.]

Probably o[n] account o[f] their larg[e] pockets, th[e] herringbon[e] twill M-194[?] trousers ar[e] worn i[n] preference t[o] the brow[n] serg[e] model. Th[e] M-193[?] gaiters an[d] the servic[e] shoes wit[h] toe caps ar[e] standar[d] issue[.]

Left.
The Quartermaster Corps had a special vest designed to meet the requirements of assault troops: made of sturdy cotton canvas this sleeveless garment has eight pockets to carry the equipment specialised soldiers such as engineers need (explosive charges etc). This vest was more practical and had better carrying and access capacity than standard equipment. The close fit of the vest enables the soldier to run and crawl more easily than when burdened with cumbersome bags and satchels. Available in three sizes: 'small', 'medium' and 'large', the vest is secured and adjusted by means of two straps. The same buckle and strap arrangement is used to seal the large pockets. The vest can be unfastened easily for access into the pockets and quicker release to avoid drowning. The vest pictured was manufactured by J.A. Shoe in 1944 as shown by the black stamp inked on the flap of the back pocket.

ORMANDY, 1944

The wide vertical stripe on the back of the M-1 helmet indicates an officer.

Right.
On the shoulders, quick release straps are connected to the suspenders of additional bags or, as here, to the gasmask haversack. The inner side of the upper compartment has a sheath to carry a bayonet or a long object. The lower front pockets have a plain flap and are used to carry either a block of TNT or a hand grenade.

The assault vest features a large back compartment of roughly the same carrying capacity as the M-1928 haversack. Sewn onto the flap is a large tab fitted with two eyeholes which help to fasten an entrenching tool (here an M-1943) the handle of which is secured by a standard buckled strap arrangement). The lower compartment at waist level has the same capacity as the M-1936 field bag. The M-1942 first-aid kit, the M-1910 canteen and the M-3 combat knife are suspended from the back of the M-1936 pistol belt.

Right.
Over the top lies a waterproof cover used to protect small arms while wading during amphibious operations. The picture also shows some items used by American engineers. Below right: an electrical exploder; left: an M-1 pull igniter; above: two time pencils next to a 200g plastic block. Above: coils of detonating (white) and priming (black) cord, with pliers. Top: a block of TNT (500g). Left and centre: two types of explosive devices laid by the Germans on the beaches: a Stockmine with ZZ35 fuse and a French 81mm mortar shell with pressure fuse. Insignia: Amphibious Training Command (a seahorse) worn on the chest pocket, and Army Engineers Combat Battalions. Both were only worn on service uniforms.

US PARATROOPER, OP

By Michel de Trez

15 August 1944 on several Italian airfields near Rome: more than 9,000 paratroopers are fitting their equipment before boarding the aircraft that will fly them to the Argens valley. The 1st Airborne Task Force was made up of various units which had fought in Italy. Interestingly, this paratrooper's steel helmet displays two different camouflage patterns: found after the war at Roquebrune-sur-Argens, this piece sports the early 'Italian pattern' of wavy brown stripes complemented by light green blotches applied before 'Dragoon'. A wide meshed net is added for securing foliage. The M 1936 suspenders have been modified by the addition of felt padding so as not to cut into the shoulders.

The paratrooper h fitted his early T-5 parachute (with wl harness) before boarding the aircr. The USAAF B-3 lif preserver is worn underneath. A sma brown platic wrist compass is fasten to the life preserve while an M-1936 fi bag is secured to harness under the reserve 'chute.

On 15 August 1944, the US Seventh Army made an amphibious landing on the French Riviera between Hyères and Cannes. Codenamed 'Dragoon', this operation called for a massive drop of paratroopers whose mission was to secure the roads and keep German reinforcements from reaching the beachhead.

Suspended from the M-1923 cartridge belt are (from left to right): a compass in its pouch; the light gas mask (training model) tied to the belt and fastened to the leg, and a locally made field dressing pocket.

Another thing typical disposition of 'Dragoon' was the improvised helmet cover made of camouflage parachute cloth. The helmet shown here has the early type of liner with chinstraps of light tan web and small brass securing studs. Carried in a pocket under the jacket collar, the small M-2 knife is secured with a plaited lanyard. The locally-made identification national flag patch is attached to the sleeve by two safety pins.

The M-1 rifle has been disassembled into its three main components and is carried in a padded canvas valise which seals with a sturdy front zipper. During the drop, the front of the valise is secured to the top right part of the harness by a snaphook.

Careful coiled, 30ft rop is tied t the belt will con in hand to see tl paratro er out o tight spots!

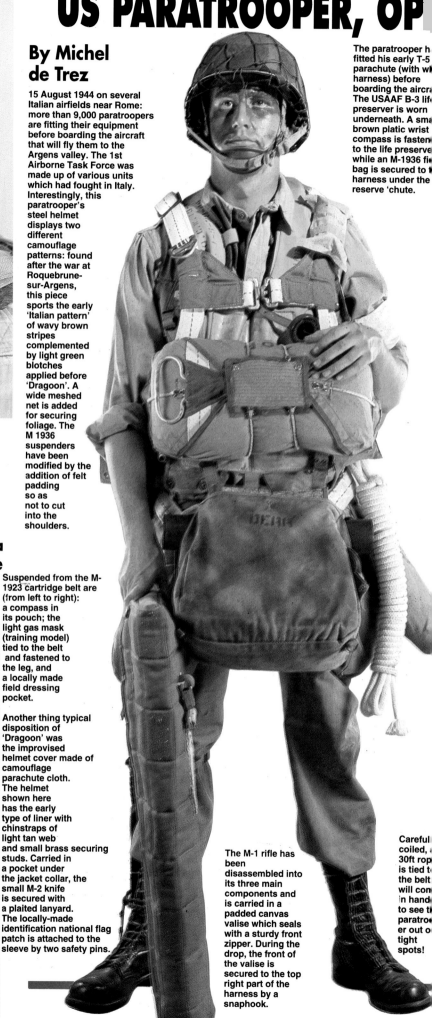

TION 'DRAGOON', 1944

To prevent untimely priming in the heat of tion, the safety lever of the Mk II hand grenade hooked on the suspenders is secured with tape.

In action, the chin piece and its straps are unclipped and folded back into the helmet liner.

Spraying garments with paint and smearing one's face with camouflage cream was a widespread practice among 1st Airborne Task Force units. The uniform's trousers and jacket are M-1942 standard US airborne issue worn with rubber heeled jump boots. The garments have been sprayed with a random pattern of green and brown blotches. The sleeves are rolled up because of the heat and no insignia are visible.

The M-1936 field bag filled with rations and personal items is secured to the suspenders. It has been sprayed with paint like the M-1910 canteen cover and the M-1943 entrenching tool cover. A strap with eyelets has been added to the bag side on which to hook extra items.

A silk map of France provides the background for two different, locally-made national flag shoulder patches, a vitaminized chocolate bar (D Ration), a knuckleduster and a Presto M-2 switchblade knife (manufactured by the George Schrade Company).

The paratrooper's special first-aid kit is tied to the left leg. An M-3 knife in its M-6 leather sheath is fastened to the right ankle.

The peculiar lacing of the Wings-skytrooper jump boots is noteworthy.

The standard steel helmet was not designed to be worn over headphones, which resulted in a poor fit. Consequently many operators did not wear the headphones, and instead kept the handset near their head so they could hear if anyone was calling them.

The T-45 'lip mic' was a special microphone used when the operator needed to have his hands free. It was not commonly used in infantry units where the radio operator was usually not the person using the microphone. The transmitting switch on the small box hung around the neck could be locked into the transmit position. The T-45 was frequently used when the BC-1000 radio was carried inside tanks to allow crews to communicate with accompanying infantry units. This mike efficiently cancelled background noise enabling the operator's voice to be heard clearly.

The M-1943 field jacket was the replace for all previous types of jackets and coa was designed to be worn over the wo 'Ike' jacket. Soldiers preferred to kee Ike jacket for dress purposes, and ins wore layers of wool shirts and swe under their M-
The radio operator has the ty appearance of American soldiers d the closing stages of the Euro conflict: his attire is a combinati early and late issue items such a standard serge trousers worn here combat boots. The double b combat boots universally like all Ame troops. repl advantaged the cumbers leggings earlier in the Although t boots designed in the troo Northern Eu didn't get until the e

No items as cant or firs pou cou suspe fron specia used wit SCR-300 the ope would norr wear a belt in additio such purp Most oper were armed wi 1 carbines but r preferred the he M-1 Garand f greater accuracy p

The BG-150 bag has pockets to hold the har as well as the short and antennae. It has two l which can be slipped any kind of belt. US S Corps bags were al designated as 'BG' as any Signal C straps were called

By Jon GAWNE

NOTHING is as important on the battlefield as good communications. With a reliable radio, one man can direct artillery and air strikes, call for reinforcements or keep track of friendly units.

The SCR-300 (Set, Complete, Radio) was the main tactical radio used by the US Army in World War 2. With an average range of three miles, it was regarded as an amazing piece of equipment for the time. Each infantry battalion had six of them: one for the CO (commanding officer), XO (executive officer) and the four company commanders. The radio operator would carry the set, and monitor the assigned channel all the time staying close to his officer.

Radio controls
The metal cover can be closed to leave only the antenna, microphones and headphone connections exposed. The small wire running to the antenna is the earthing wire used to make up for the difference in length of the two antennae. The handset plugs into the two jacks on the left, while the single jack next to the antenna is used for the headset. A special relay can be plugged into the top left jack so that the radio can be remotely operated (for example from the cellar when the set is on the top floor of a house).
All jacks are covered with a waterproof spring-loaded rubber plug when not in use. The channel selector in the centre can be tuned to any of 41 different channels, and then locked in place by a knob.

UROPE, 1944-1945

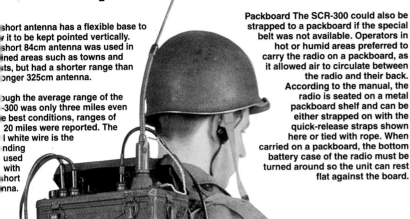

short antenna has a flexible base to
w it to be kept pointed vertically.
short 84cm antenna was used in
ned areas such as towns and
sts, but had a shorter range than
onger 325cm antenna.

ough the average range of the
-300 was only three miles even
e best conditions, ranges of
20 miles were reported. The
l white wire is the
nding
used
with
hort
nna.

Packboard The SCR-300 could also be
strapped to a packboard if the special
belt was not available. Operators in
hot or humid areas preferred to
carry the radio on a packboard, as
it allowed air to circulate between
the radio and their back.
According to the manual, the
radio is seated on a metal
packboard shelf and can be
either strapped on with the
quick-release straps shown
here or tied with rope. When
carried on a packboard, the
bottom battery case of the radio must be
turned around so the unit can rest
flat against the board.

Radio and accessories
The three parts of the
special SCR-300 harness
are the backpad (M-391),
the belt (ST-55) and the
harness (ST-54). The
accessories (from left to
right) are: the long
antenna (AN-131); BG-
150 bag; TS-15
handset; AN-130
short antenna and
HS-30 headset.
The radio itself was
designated as BC-
1000 and - as pictured here with its
accessories - was called the SCR-
300. It weighed 17kg with battery.
When used in a tank, the complete
set would be called an AN/VRC-3.
The SCR-300 was colloquially
known as a 'Walkie-Talkie' in
World War 2. The smaller hand-
held SCR-536 was referred to as a
'Handie-Talkie', and used mostly
for communications between the
different platoons of a company. Its
range however was so short that
most soldiers regarded it as
useless.
The SCR-300 and SCR-536
operated on different principles
(Frequency Modulation and Amplitude
Modulation) and were not compatible.

top
tion of the
carries the
eiver/transmitter
while the
er bottom
tion is the
ery holder.
teries
erally had a
our
rational life
weighed
ost as
ch as the
smitter.

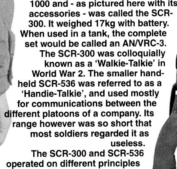

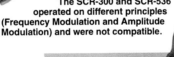

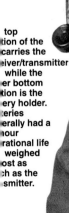

99

AMERICAN MEDIC

This medic has managed to secure the warmest garments he could lay his hands on, and combined them into a snug - if somewhat unaesthetic - outfit. The typical Medical Issue Litter Carrying Suspenders and pouch are particularly noteworthy.

His hands are protected by woollen mittens which are best suited to operations involving careful and delicate handling.

TWO nasty shocks were in store for the Americans when they liberated the Ardennes in late 1944: first the German counter-offensive which caught them totally unawares and then the bitter cold.

But while US Army commanders devised a plan to check the nazi onslaught, soldiers out in the field had to cope with the weather and solve everyday living problems. Throughout this protracted battle, the GIs made the most of their proverbial assets: ingenuity and resourcefulness.

This private is clad in a model Mackinaw w unlined collar. The ma kitted out in the typ equipment issue American medics on European front: helmet is adorned w four red cros painted on a wi background (repea the pattern of armban

The left-hand pouch contains:
- Eight individual field dressings (one is open to show its contents).
- One Book, Emergency Medical Tag, displayed on an armband. Each tag is a questionnaire that must be filled in to give the particulars of the wounds. It can be tied to the patient's clothing by a piece of string. A carbon copy of the medical report is kept in the book.
- One lead pencil.
- Two carrying straps.
Two regulation armbands are shown: a red cross is sewn on one side and on the other, a stamp stipulates that the wearer is protected by the Geneva Convention. The medic's personal number also appears on the armband (inked on the top model and stamped on the bottom one).

'Trouse Comb Winte heavy w padd trouse

Oversho Arc made can a rubb they faster by fe metal hoo Worn o stand service sho they keep feet dry slush a sn

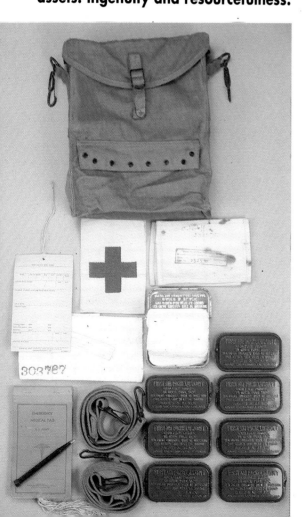

rn
cher
).
teel
are
with
en
les
teel
ps.

ARDENNES, 1944

By Jacques ALLUCHON

The back view shows clearly the width of the special harness. It can be used to carry a stretcher or tow a small cart. A small strap identical to the front one connects the suspenders and secures the pouches. These straps keep the pouches securely in place and can also double as pouch handles when the harness is not in use.

Combined use of carrying suspenders with webbing. Each strap is fastened to the front and rear handles of the suspenders. The shafts of the stretcher fit in the loops, easing off the weight and spreading the load more evenly.

Contents of the right-hand pouch:
- tourniquet
- plaster, adhesive
- safety pins
- scissors
- eye injury set
- burn injury set
- iodine swabs
- metal container holding 12 iodine swabs
- bandages (several types)

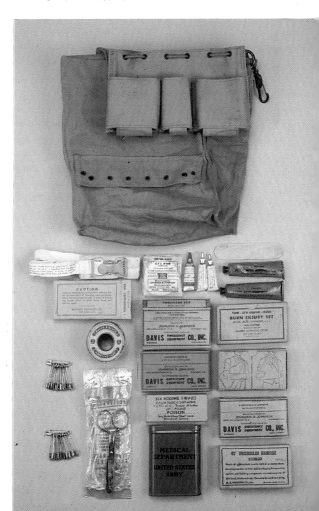

Left.
This private from 23rd Armored Infantry Battalion is ready for the assault. His impedimenta are restricted to the bare necessities. Because of isolation and lack of adequate clothing, the unit, like many others, had been issued with British snow camouflage overalls. This garment was worn over the winter combat uniform which made ample provision for woollen undergarments. The US M1 helmet is worn over the woolknit cap, itself designed to fit under the liner.

Over the thick cotton hooded overall, the GI wears M-1936 suspenders with a BAR M-1937 magazine belt that holds 12 magazines. An 1917 Pattern bandoleer holds an additional six spare magazines. The hands are protected with standard woollen gloves with leather palm reinforcements.

FROM 18 to 22 December 1944, American soldiers from the 7th Armored Division and 14th Cavalry Group were involved in a bitter struggle to slow down the German advance sweeping through the streets of St Vith, a small village in the Ardennes. Having outrun their supply columns in the fast thrust of the previous weeks, these GIs found themselves deprived of adequate equipment when winter set in.

By Jacques ALLUCHON

The matching trousers have one large patch pocket on the right leg. Footwear consists of 'Shoe pac, 12 inch', with rubber lowers and leather uppers. Unlike the older rubber and canvas overshoes, Shoepacs were suitable for long walks and usually worn with two pairs of woollen socks plus one or two insulating fibre insoles.

Left.
Close-up on the windjacket and trousers. The windjacket fastens by means of hood and bottom drawstrings. The trousers have a similar device at the waist. The pockets of both garments have buttoned flaps (only the windjacket pockets have plaits). For improved camouflage, the trouser legs can be worn loose over the boots.
The trousers and pleated chest pockets have buttoned flaps. The bottom of the trousers legs and the sleeves are loose. The British markings are conspicuous, and the brown plastic buttons stand out on the unlined snow overall.

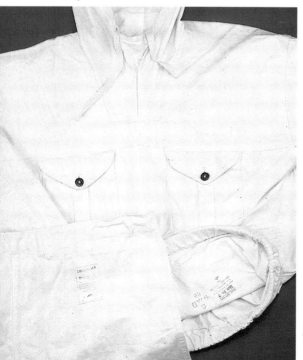

RDENNES 1944

Right
The man has lowered his hood during a pause, showing the M-1941 wool knit 'beanie' folded down over his ears to protect them from the cold. The regulation olive drab woollen scarf had been loosened. Also showing is the wide tightening strap at the bottom of the windjacket.

The efficiency of the camouflage is well conveyed in this back view showing the GI with the hood up. To avoid confusion with German soldiers who had a similar snow camouflage outfit, a brightly coloured circle was often painted on the back. An M-3 knife and the regulation issue canteen are suspended from the belt.

Rigth.
Displayed on the windjacket are the woollen scarf (above left) and the obverse side of the BAR ammunition belt showing the manufacturer's stencils (Boyt). Below, the popular woolknit beanie and the 'Gloves, wool, olive drab, leather palm' displayed so as to show both sides. The boots were highly sought after by soldiers and the close-up shows the markings painted inside the cuff as well as the size indicated between the heel and the sole.

Left. The 1942 Pattern one-piece suit. Made of HBT cloth, this garment was originally meant for mechanics but also issued to soldiers on jungle duty and tank crews. The pockets, two on the chest, two on the back, and two on the sides are noteworthy. The side pockets had a slit opening so as to provide access to the trouser pockets. The buttons were made of metal. A fastening strap was placed on the bottom leg. The HBT cap was made of light green HBT cloth, the typical green colour of which matched the uniform.

Right. The 1943 Pattern one-piece herringbone outfit worn with a cap made of similar cloth. The new colour, deeper than the previous green hue, is conspicuous.

Below. The 1942 Pattern combat jacket worn with the small HBT hat. Initially meant for training and fatigues, this uniform was also worn in the jungle. The metal buttons are noteworthy.

1941-45 US ARMY HERRINGBONE TWILL AND JUNGLE OUTFITS

By Jacques ALLUCHON

On the eve of Pearl Harbor, the 'dough-boy's' uniform was the standard 1908 Pattern outfit made of the famous 'blue denim' which had replaced the brown cloth in 1919. Improved in 1940, this garment was worn until supplies ran out, a practice which was more prevalent in the far-flung garrisons of the Pacific and in the Philippines than among other units. However, some Americans soldiers posted to Great Britain in 1942 still wore that uniform.

A one-piece overall made of blue denim was introduced in 1933 for mechanics and drivers. It proved unsatisfactory though, and was soon replaced with a new model based on the model issued to Air Corps mechanics. For its manufacture, another cloth had been selected: a thickly woven cotton with a peculiar fishbone-like weave colloquially known as herringbone twill or HBT. Dyed olive drab, this

cloth was used for the manufacture of US working suits until 1945.

In May 1941, the War Department announced that the blue denim outfits were to be superseded with olive green herringbone twill models.

The 1942 Pattern

The new HBT outfit was manufactured according to specifications issued in 1942. Originally it was meant for mechanics and tank crews, while another two-piece model was distributed to other personnel for wear as a fatigue and training outfit. The trousers were patterned from the serge service model, while the tunic, shaped like a long blouse, was cut with greater care than the denim version.

The manufacture of the HBT fatigues started in the autumn of 1942. On issue during the early stages of the Pacific campaign and

in North Africa, these fatigues were hardly worn in the European theatre. Although widely distributed to infantry officers and all ranks serving in the Pacific, the fatigues officially remained the hallmark of tank crews. In Tunisia, they were worn over the woollen uniform and occasionally with the lined winter combat jacket.

But the operational wear of HBT outfits was short-lived: they were manufactured until new suits were introduced in 1943. These fatigues had a simplified design and were better suited to military duties than the previous uniforms.

The 1943 Outfit

The new, simplified outfit had now become a genuine combat uniform with anti-vesicatory properties. The watertightness of some 'Special' models were improved after being

Left.
A 1st Cavalry Division trooper in Leyte, Philippines, in October 1944. He is clad in the 1943 Pattern herringbone twill suit with plastic buttons. Soldiers of this unit often preferred to wear a cap than a steel helmet. The boots of the early pattern were made of leather and canvas. They were a good substitute for standard combat boots which rotted quickly in the jungle. The simplifed cut of the jacket is noteworthy. It could be worn like a tunic or tucked into the trousers. The cargo pockets have a central pleat, a variant left to the care of manufacturers in February 1943. The camouflage cloth jungle pack is strapped on. The straps used to secure the pack to the belt were identical to those fitted on the M-1928 Pattern haversack. Often, one of the smaller front 'Y' staps was cut off. The weapon is an US M-1. Magazines are carried in the twin pouches slipped onto the web belt from which a fighting knife hangs.

Right.
May 1945: officer of the 37th Infantry Division in Manila. His uniform is devoid of badges and insignia. The 1943 Pattern Herringbone HBT combat uniform has metal buttons. The tropical boots were introduced in the closing stages of the conflict. Made of leather and canvas, they were sturdier than those worn by the soldier at left. A jungle first aid kit and a M-1942 pouch are suspended from the belt.
The varying shades of the uniform are noteworthy: the jacket has faded into a lighter shade of olive drab. The helmet chin straps are hanging loose.

made 'protective' by a further chemical treatment.

Mass production began in 1942. Known as Olive Drab N°7, a new dark green colour was selected later that year and used to dye herringbone twill outfits and individual web equipment.

The one-piece suit was similar to a civilian boiler suit. Most of the pockets were under the waist; and the back comfort darts were dropped. The hip and side trouser pockets of the two-piece uniform were replaced with a cargo pocket on each leg.

The jacket (as defined in the 1942 regulations) was cut like a long and loose fitting shirt. Its two large pleated chest pockets were identical to the trousers'. Some HBT uniforms even had plastic buttons which didn't rot in humid jungle conditions.

The 1943 Two-Piece Herringbone Twill Suit was worn throughout the 1943-45 Europe and Pacific campaigns, and was still issued when the Korean War broke out a few years later. The suit was worn on its own in summertime and over woollen undergarments in cold weather.

Theoretically, the overall was only issued to mechanics and tank crews.

The US Army HBT suit was followed by the cotton Olive Gren 107 which was introduced in the 1950s.

Headgear

Along with the blue denim, a small rounded hat was introduced but soon replaced by a cap. Later, HBT cloth was used for its manufacture. Tha cap was issued to armoured forces personnel but frequently worn by infantrymen. A later version manufactured in 1945 had a larger peak.

Jungle Uniforms
By 1942, strong demand from the Pacific theatre resulted in the HBT being adopted as the standard jungle uniform. It repaced the light tan Chino suit and trousers on regular issue in the prewar years which was discontinued after the Philippines campaign. However, to meet with the requirements issued by the US Quartermaster Corps, a genuine jungle combat uniform was designed, while research was being conducted so its colours would match Pacific surroundings. The camouflage colours were those predominently associated with the Pacific battlefields: on one side, the pattern consisted of various shades of

brown which blended with the colours of landing beaches, while the other sported the predominently greenish colours of the rain forest.

In July 1942, 150,000 tropical uniforms were ordered in advance for the upcoming offensives in the Solomon Islands and New Guinea. The emergency led to a stop-gap measure being adopted in the shape of a camouflage overall, worn directly on the skin for better ventilation. This uniform became standard issue in 1942.

In addition to its camouflage properties, the overall had to protect against insects and also provide good ventilation. Loose fitting, it had wide hip and chest pockets. However, extensive wear showed that the one-piece suit was cumbersome, too hot for south Pacific conditions and proved particularly awkward when a soldier had to relieve himself.

A new two-piece model was found to be preferable and thus, the 1942 Pattern two-piece suit was designed and widely issued. It was soon replaced with another model which could be manufactured even quicker.

In May 1943, a camouflage two-piece HBT suit was adopted. The shirt was made of the same camouflage cloth as the one-piece overall but, because of its cut, was not reversible.

1 Jungle pack.
2 M-1943 Pack with strapped machete and poncho. The pack is made of olive drab cloth. The pack flap has an inner zipped pocket.
3 Band, Helmet, Camouflage to affix foliage and twigs to the steel helmet.
4 HBT cap sporting the 6th Infantry Division insignia.
5 Jungle, Firts Aid Kit, carried on the belt (slipped on or suspended).
6 Bladder, Flotation, Jungle. A set of two bladders was slipped under the jacket for river crossings. Insignia issued to some of the units deployed in the Pacific are deployed on the bladder (these insignia were not worn on the HBT uniform): 7th ID, 24th ID, 25th ID and the Americal Division.
7 Bulova issue watch.
8 Regular issue compass in waterproofed bag.
9 Mosquito net.
10 Conversation handbook.
11 M-1944 mosquito net (worn on the head or over the helmet).
12 Japanese pay book and American songbook.

Far left.
infantryman of 41st Armoured Infantry Regiment in Normandy, June 1944. A few units deployed in Normandy were issued with two-piece jungle camouflage uniforms. This uniform was not reversible although both sides had a different camouflage pattern (buttons and pockets were on the darker side only).

Left. **An NCO of 25th ID in Guadalcanal in December 1942. The new cjungle suit is loose-fitting for improved ventilation. The uniform is worn with open collar; the sleeves and trouser legs are rolled up. A long zipper runs down the front. Inner suspenders ease off the weight of the large hip and chest pockets. The helmet cover never went past the experimental stage. The man is armed with an M-1928 submachine-gun. A spare drum magazine is carried in the bag slung over the man's shoulder.**

Both jacket and trousers were patterned on the 1943 two-piece HBT uniform but included a few modifications: buttons for braces, cargo pockets with wider openings, elbow and knee reinforcements, and plastic buttons. The button holes were protected with flaps to keep twigs out. The two piece jungle suit had a chest cape and bellowed fly and cuffs for protection against combat gasses.

But the efficiency of the camouflage and the suitablity of the HBT materiel were questioned after testing in actual combat conditions had shown that in addition to drying slowly, the cloth became heavy and lost its windproof properties when soaked - two drawbacks which considerably worsened a soldier's lot. Besides, camouflage only made a soldier less conspicuous as long as he lay motionless - resulting in much the reverse effect being achieved when he was on the move. A neutral colour such as grey-green was found to be more discreet in the field. These drawbacks led to camouflage clothing being phased out by March 1944. The N°7 Olive Drab HBT uniform introduced in 1943 became regular issue for troops deployed in the jungle.

Meanwhile, experiments led to a new cloth, the Oxford poplin cotton, being selected for the manufacture of uniforms. After many field tests, a new combat uniform made of this material was adopted in July 1945. With five buttons down the front, the jacket had an anti-gas cape and two small chest patch pockets sealing with a buttoned flap. The trousers had two front patch pockets and two flapped ones at the back. The bottom of the legs were secured around the boots with hemmed laces.

Headgear and Individual Equipment

The standard headgear was the M-1 steel helmet, often worn without its cloth cover. A camouflage cloth reversible cover had been introduced in 1942 but never issued. A liner sprayed with camouflage paint was also tested but soon dropped. Instead, a wide elasticated strap for affixing foliage was widely used. In the field, the helmet was often replaced by a hat, and later by an HBT cap. A fibre helmet - theorically phased out in 1942 - was issued to rear echelon troops.

American soldiers deployed in the Pacific theatre received the same equipment as other troops but were none-the-less issued with items specifically designed for jungle conditions. The most noticeable among them was the 'jungle pack' made of watertight camouflage cloth.

Meant to supersede the standard issue M-1928 haversack, the pack was also available in green canvas and widely issued to American troops deployed in the European theatre. Soldiers deployed in the jungle were also issued with machetes and compasses as well as flotation bags for river crossing river.

For protection against bad weather, troops had raincoats and were issued in 1943 with a large poncho (originally made of green nylon, these ponchos were later manufactured in rubberised canvas).

To fend off malaria in insect ridden regions, the GIs had mosquito nets and cotton gloves as well as a special hammock with its own mosquito net.

For basic health care, the Medical Department evolved a first aid kit which was introduced in 1943. Slipped or hooked on the belt, these kits contained foot lotion, insect repellent, standard field dressings, tablets, band aids, and burn ointment.

US MARINE GUADALCANA

This Marine (equivalent to private in the US Army) has just been issued with an US-M1 helmet, with square welded chinstrap loops and cloth-covered cardboard liner. Introduced in 1940, the dog tag was worn singly until 1943 and slipped on a leather thong. The 'Chino' shirt is cut differently from the Army model. The M-1941 haversack on which the soldier has fastened his M-1942 bayonet in its M-1912 scabbard is also a recent issue.

ON 7 August 1942, the 1st Marine Division landed on Guadalcanal and quickly overcame Japanese resistance. But prompt and violent Japanese air attacks soon interfered with the operation. Marines taking part in this action still wore the 'Chino' fatigues, a summer outfit that was being replaced gradually by the green Herringone Twill Utilities on specific issue to the Corps.

The standard weapon is still the M-1903 Springfield rifle, that remained in service with the Marine Corps until October 1943 when gradually replaced by the Garand. The sling was made of canvas, a material better suited to jungle conditions than leather. The M1918 chest grenade carrier was replaced in 1943 by the M1 Ammunition Bag. Made of sturdy drab canvas, the rig consisted of two rows of five pouches each sealing with studs and holding 10 smok, chemical or Mk II hand grenades. One of the fragmentation grenades protrudes from one of the pouches, showing its yellow finish. From mid-1942 onwards, grenades were coated with olive drab paint but existing stocks were used up in the original colour.

Close up of the shirt and trousers showing the particular pointed pocket flaps and the white reinforcement front strip bearing the buttonholes. The typical reddish brown buttons also differentiate this shirt from the army model. Originally, both shirt and trousers had the same colour but extensive wear and washing make the shirt looks much lighter than the mint trousers shown here.

The standard iss M1923 cartridge has 10 pouches; 26inch N°128 Co Legitimus mach hangs in its leatl sheath with etch markings.

Made of the sam Chino material a shirt, the trouser lack the typical pocket of the Ar model.

ECEMBER 1942

By
**Jacques
ALLUCHON**

pical USMC issue,
M-1910
enching tool
er has no
kings while its
ks are farther apart
on Army models.
canvas also has a
ser texture.

The canteen
cloth cover is
ned and fitted
h 'lift the dot'
essure studs.
The stencilled
ures indicate
at this Marine
elongs to the
1st Co. of the
d Regiment's
3rd Battalion.

Standard issue
M-1942 field
dressing
pocket.

The M-1942 bayonet is not
so well crafted as the M-
1905 Pattern: its blade is
parkerised instead of
polished, and brown or
black bakelite has been
substituted to wood for the
handle plates. The
sophisticated M-1910
sheath is made of two
wooden parts held
together by leather lacing
and secured in a thick
canvas sheath featuring
the attaching hook.
Although manufactured in
1943, the Collins
Legitimus machete is a
World War One design,
with a steel reinforced
leather scabbard that was
quickly discarded and
replaced by plain canvas
models, better suited to
the humid conditions
where they were used.

MERRILL'S MARAUDER

September 1944: a 'Merrill's Marauder' veteran poses for the photographer at the unit's rear base in India. The man now belongs to the 475th Infantry Regiment which has retained the traditions of Merrill's unit. On the sleeve of the summer cotton shirt, the locally made insignia worn by troops fighting in the China-India-Burma theatre is sewn above the First Sergeant 'stripes'. The Presidential Unit Citation (emblem awarded for the capture of Myitkyina) is pinned above the right chest pocket; the Combat Infantryman Badge, the ribbons for the Bronze Star (for gallantry), the American Campaign Medal and the Asiatic-Pacific Campaign Medal with a bronze star for the Burma campaign are worn on the left side of the chest. The summer garrison cap is piped in the light blue colour of the infantry.

Unlik
Japanese
Marau
had
helm
with
camouflag
scrimma
avoid confus
The paint o
soldier's US
helmet is alr
weathered an
chinstrap has ro
a

To ease the we
off his should
the man le
forward and
on the
straps o
havers

weapo
an
Gar

The combat outfit is the Pattern 1943 herringbone twill fatigue dress, with large chest and leg cargo pockets. The jacket tucked into the trousers is devoid of rank insignia. The standard individual equipment consists of an M-1923 cartridge belt supporting two canteens and a field dressing pocket. Only worn on dry ground and surfaced roads, the service shoes are strapped to the M-1928 haversack next to the waterproof poncho. The mess kit pouch is full of tins and hangs next to the 1910 Pattern folding entrenching tool. The haversack holds a blanket, iron rations for three to five days as well as two flotation bladders for fording rivers.

A reminder of training in India - and one of the Chindits' favourite weapons - the redoubtable Nepalese kukri is slipped into the belt.

Introduced in Aug
1942, the 'Bo
Jungle', were mo
issued to elite tro
deployed in trop
zones. Although o
soldiers tende
dislike them, m
than half of
Marauders selec
this footwear fo
sturdiness in mar
surroundings. Th
boots also d
faster and provi
better g
ventilation and stea
The quarter fastens v
laces and eyeholes, a
the shaft is laced in
same way as M-1938 v
gaiters.
manufacturer's name
Rubber Co) is stamp
inside the sh

DURING the Burma campaign, the British introduced a new concept in warfare: long range penetration units. Transported behind Japanese lines, these air-supplied columns disrupted communications and wrought havoc around the enemy's rear.

The Americans followed suit by raising a similar force to open the Ledo and Burma roads, and to link India to China. In October 1943, the *5307th Composite Regiment (Provisional)* was raised from volunteers. Trained by the famous '*Chindits*', the formation was converted into a *Composite Unit* (codenamed the *Galahad Force*) on 2 January 1944. Totalling about 3,000 men, the unit had a lighter structure (three regiments each with two *Combat Teams*), supported by two mule pack units provided by the Quartermaster Corps totalling some 700 horses and mules. To reach its departure base in Burma, the Composite Unit trekked over 250km through the jungle. It was then that its nickname '*Merrill's Marauders*' was coined by *Time/Life* correspondent James Shepley to honour its Commander, Brigadier General Frank D.Merrill.

In March 1944, the Marauders defeated Japan's elite 18th Division prior to heading for the important rear base of Myitkyina which General 'Vinegar Joe' Stillwell, the overall commander of the operation, wanted to reach before the monsoon. Forming into three parallel columns, the Marauders made for their objectives but were delayed by numerous clashes with the Japanese. The Americans had lost nearly two thirds of their men to exhaustion, disease and malnutrition before launching the assault. Assisted by two Chinese regiments, the survivors captured Myitkyina air-strip on 17 May but the city of Miytkyina did not fall until 3 August. Then, the Marauders - who had not been relieved since the beginning of the campaign - had to go through the humiliation of a medical check up ordered by Merrill who refused to believe that the disappointing performance of his men could be blamed on their poor physical condition. The surviving Marauders were commissioned with the *475th Infantry Regiment (Long Range Penetration, Special)* and attached to the *Mars Task Force* for the October 1944 drive to Burma.

URMA, 1944

by Philippe CARBONNIER
and Pierre BESNARD

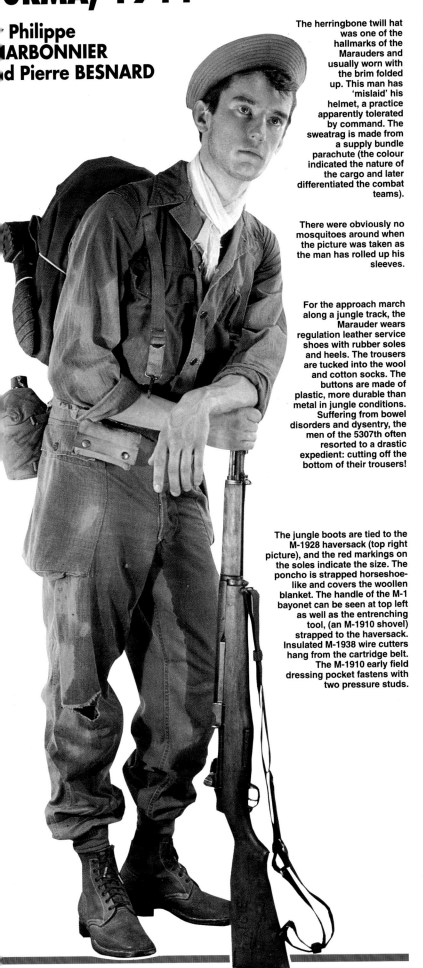

The herringbone twill hat was one of the hallmarks of the Marauders and usually worn with the brim folded up. This man has 'mislaid' his helmet, a practice apparently tolerated by command. The sweatrag is made from a supply bundle parachute (the colour indicated the nature of the cargo and later differentiated the combat teams).

There were obviously no mosquitoes around when the picture was taken as the man has rolled up his sleeves.

For the approach march along a jungle track, the Marauder wears regulation leather service shoes with rubber soles and heels. The trousers are tucked into the wool and cotton socks. The buttons are made of plastic, more durable than metal in jungle conditions. Suffering from bowel disorders and dysentery, the men of the 5307th often resorted to a drastic expedient: cutting off the bottom of their trousers!

The jungle boots are tied to the M-1928 haversack (top right picture), and the red markings on the soles indicate the size. The poncho is strapped horseshoe-like and covers the woollen blanket. The handle of the M-1 bayonet can be seen at top left as well as the entrenching tool, (an M-1910 shovel) strapped to the haversack. Insulated M-1938 wire cutters hang from the cartridge belt. The M-1910 early field dressing pocket fastens with two pressure studs.

MERRILL'S MARAUDERS' INSIGNIA

Unofficially issued, these locally-made insignia were exclusively worn in the Burma theatre.
A and B: 5307th Composite Unit (Provisional). The four colours represent four of the six combat teams (oddly the 'Khaki' and 'Orange' teams are missing from the insignia). The two stars (with respectively 12 points for China and five for the United States) symbolise the union of the two countries against Japan. Stillwell had two of Chiang Kai-Shek's divisions under his command. The lightning bolt is a symbol of power.
C and D: Mars Task Force - 5332nd Brigade (Provisional). Unofficial insignia issued to Mars Task Force - 5332nd Brigade (Provisional). Raised on 10 August in Ledo, India, this unit comprised Merrill's marauders (integrated within the 475th Infantry Regiment), the 124th Cavalry Regiment, one Chinese regiment and two US artillery battalions. The Mars Task Force was involved in the liberation of Burma in January 1945, prior to being air transported to China where it was eventually disbanded in late May 1945. The four insignia, especially the Indian-made models, vary considerably in design and manufacture.

Left. The reversible camouflage helmet cloth cover with front USMC eagle, globe and anchor emblem displays its predominently green, 'jungle' side.

Officially called 'olive drab', the herringbone twill 'utilities' had a peculiar bluish hue when new but quickly faded to a pale greyish-green. The jacket has three patch pockets without flaps (one on the left breast and one on each hip), and its front and cuffs are fastened with metallic buttons. The USMC acronym and the Marine Corps emblem are stencilled on the chest pocket.

The US M-1 steel helmet is worn with loose chinstrap and still fitted with the early type of cardboard liner. Suspended on the chest, the Colt M1911A1 pistol is carried in a brown leather M-7 shoulder holster.

This officer, a plato▶ commander, is clad▶ the two-pie▶ herringbone tv▶ utilities. This coml▶ uniform was introduc▶ in mid-1942 and beca▶ the most widely worr▶ all US Marines' coml▶ outfits. Considered as▶ dangerous invitation▶ snipers, all rank insig▶ were banned and or▶ his equipme▶ distinguishes this offi▶ from enlisted me▶

The USMC web suspenders are fastened to the back of the cartridge belt by two snaphooks, and connect to the front by simple hooks fitted at the end of 'Y' straps.

Garand M-1 rifle.

FOUGHT in the closing stages of the Pacific Campaign, the battle of Iwo Jima involved three Marine divisions and the entire 3rd Fleet. From 19 February to 26 March 1945, the 'leathernecks' were involved in a bitter struggle against the Japanese who inflicted 25,000 casualties on the Americans forces before collapsing.

Left.
USMC canteen covers are not lined with felt. This model with crossed flaps was introduced in mid-1944. The holster strap arrangement is noteworthy. Made of webbing and identical to the M1923 Army model, the cartridge belt consists of 10 pouches with snap studs, and features the USMC acronym and the manufacturer's name inked on the inner side. Interestingly, the eyelets of USMC belts are wider apart (5mm), explaining the typical warping of the M-1910 hooks on USMC web equipment. The haversack can be hooked to the middle eyelet of the cartridge belt's rear connecting strap to prevent flapping.

Canv▶ ma▶ dispatc▶ cas▶

Standard 'roug▶ side out' leath▶ boot▶

WO-JIMA 1945

anvas haversack has
n straps. The
uflage poncho is
ned horseshoe-like
ree straps. As on
1928 Army
sack, the 'T'-
ed Army issue
nching tool and
ayonet (not shown
are fastened by
ooks.

e out of
ame
rial as
cket, the
ers have
lanted
pockets
out
) and two
atch
ets.
Pacific,
ers were
worn
e or
over
eggings.

By Jacques ALLUCHON

Right.
Like the helmet cover, the rubberised camouflage poncho is reversible and is shown here in its mottled 'beach' pattern in various shades of brown. The green 'jungle' side is generally darker. The poncho fastens around the neck with pressure studs.

Hanging from the belt over the right hip, the 'Jungle First Aid Pouch' is seen next to standard M1910 field dressing pocket that is still on issue to the Marine Corps.

Right.
The centrepiece of this composition is the famous KA-BAR Bowie Knife, the indispensible companion of the 'leathernecks'. The hidden side of the blade carries the Marine Corps markings. The short flapped, fabric canteen cover sports the geometric marking of the 4th Marine Division ('5' stands for the regiment, '2' for the battalion, and '4' for the company).The USMC answered to the Navy and was accordingly issued with Navy pattern boots and field dressings (bottom). The web leggings and the camouflage shelter half (the label of which is visible just under a boot) are on specific issue to the Corps. The stamps on the map folder (top) are noteworthy. The M1938 compass (bottom left) was on general issue to US Armed Forces.

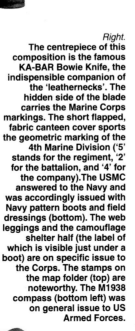

Left. The harness is strapped on, and the parachute bag hooked to the chest buckles. The ripcord runs along the parachute strap. The AN-R2 raft is fastened to the Mae West's metal buckle by a sling.

In strict compliance with US Navy directives, no rank or unit badges appear on the one-piece flying suit of the officer commanding VF3 Fighter Squadron. Only a small brown leather tab with name and rank is sewn on the left side of the chest. The M-426A light cotton flying suit was adopted by the Navy in the prewar years and was worn throughout the conflict. Complete lack of outer chest pockets was one of the suit's pecularities (access to these pockets would have been denied by the Mae West). The legs have two large cargo pockets sealing with pressure studs, while the chest features an inner pocket for personal documents and small items. Two zipped slits grant access to the pockets of the trousers which could be worn under the flying suit. The bottoms of the legs fasten with zippers. In addition to the lack of outer chest pockets and the quality of its manufacture, the outfit is characterised by two large diamond-shaped reinforcements made of matching material on each arm. The parachute harness and the survival kit are clipped on just before boarding the aircraft.

The 'flesh out' leather shoes are standard US Navy issue.

BY Jacques ALLUCHON

November 1943. As dawn breaks off Bougainville, the northermost island of the Solomon archipelago, mechanics are revving up the engines of the F-4F Wildcats lined up on the deck of the USS Saratoga. After the briefing, the pilots file out of the 'Ready Room' and proceed to their aircraft. Soon, they will participate in Operation 'Cherry Blossom', involving the landing at Empress Augusta Bay of the 3rd Marine Division, supported by the 23rd (American) and 37th Infantry Divisions. Following the recapture of New Georgia two months previously, 'Cherry Blossom' is the next step in the reconquest of the South Pacific.

-592 survival kit is strapped
the parachute back pad. It is
d like a knapsack above the
Vest but under the
hute strap so as not to be
hen the pilot slips out of
rness after ditching. The kit
ened by two wide cotton
slung over the shoulders
eld together by a chest
The typical Mae West
stencils are noteworthy.
clusive issue to Navy
, the QAS (Quick
nable Seat) parachute
sts of a harness
rn on the pilot) and
chute pack,
the aircraft seat
tored under the
2 inflatable raft.
e a flight, the
hooks together
arness and
rge loops
rotrude
the
hute pack,
e two
er
hute

hooks

ss

es.

lex

gement
chosen
ease of
se,
ned to
ent the
rom
dragged
bottom
s
logged
y. Through
mple
dient of
ing two
hooks, the
can get rid of
py, harness
ines. This
ion was
d to be
rable to
ing the
hooks of
ght fitting
ess, which
also
with other
s of kit.

Right.
The parachute is shown here
fastened to the harness. The
raft bag is held cushion-like
under the parachute pack.
Tightly packed in a canvas bag,
the raft and its accessories
were about as comfortable as a
wooden board! The metal
shrouded ripcord cable runs
along the strap connecting the
parachute pack to the harness
front.

Two ID tags
issueto Harold
K. Hughes. The
early 1917
Pattern shows
the rank of junior
lieutenant and
that its wearer
was born before 1940. The lieutenant
commander's tag was crafted in
September 1941 and carries his
etched finger print on its obverse
side, a practice which was
discontinued in December 1942. This
tag indicates that the reserve
Lieutenant Junior Grade was a student
pilot who was commissioned with the
Navy after completing training in 1940.
The 1941 tag indicates that the man has
been promoted to the rank of lieutenant
commander in the meantime. (US Navy
personnel are issued with new dog tags
after each promotion.) Thanks to his
former reservist status, Hughes could
enlist before reaching the age of 21.
This ploy enabled the US Navy and the
USMC to select men of their choice
before Army call-up. Although
controversial, this practice was retained
until 1943 when the military authorities
forced the Navy to give up - at least
partially - this unusual recruiting
procedure.

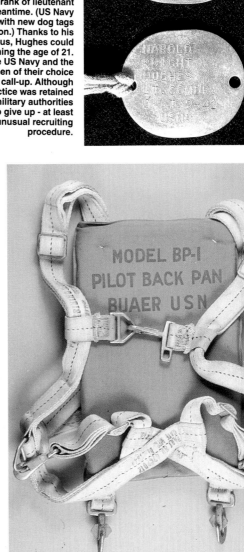

Right.
Close up of harness and
back pad stencils. The
harness and canopy are
manufactured by Switlik.
The manufacturer's
particulars and the
production date are
stencilled under the bottom
straps of the harness.
Fitted with a large eyelet
connecting to the
parachute pack strap, the
chest springhook is
clearly visible. The
parachute shown here
was phased out after the
war according to the
'Final Striking Date Oct
1953' indication. The
seat cushion's upper
half is rigid, while the
lower part carries on its
inner side the particulars
of the model. BUAER
stands for Bureau of
Aeronautics, the official
body tasked with defining
the specifications of US
naval equipment.

PILOTE DE LA VF3, *USS SARATOGA, 1943*

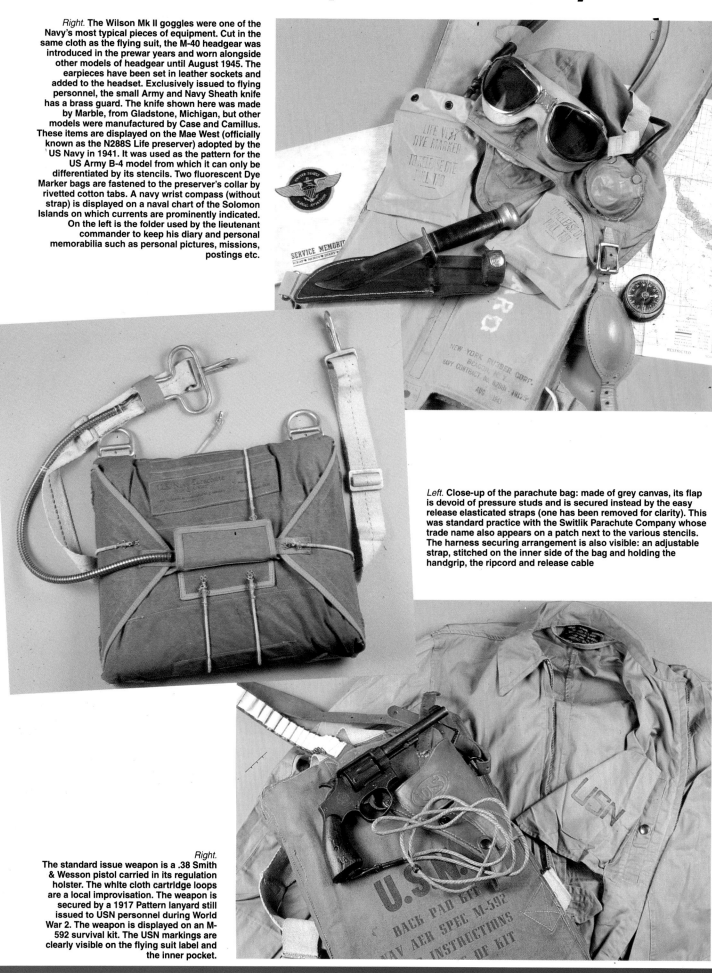

Right. The Wilson Mk II goggles were one of the Navy's most typical pieces of equipment. Cut in the same cloth as the flying suit, the M-40 headgear was introduced in the prewar years and worn alongside other models of headgear until August 1945. The earpieces have been set in leather sockets and added to the headset. Exclusively issued to flying personnel, the small Army and Navy Sheath knife has a brass guard. The knife shown here was made by Marble, from Gladstone, Michigan, but other models were manufactured by Case and Camillus. These items are displayed on the Mae West (officially known as the N288S Life preserver) adopted by the US Navy in 1941. It was used as the pattern for the US Army B-4 model from which it can only be differentiated by its stencils. Two fluorescent Dye Marker bags are fastened to the preserver's collar by rivetted cotton tabs. A navy wrist compass (without strap) is displayed on a naval chart of the Solomon Islands on which currents are prominently indicated. On the left is the folder used by the lieutenant commander to keep his diary and personal memorabilia such as personal pictures, missions, postings etc.

Left. Close-up of the parachute bag: made of grey canvas, its flap is devoid of pressure studs and is secured instead by the easy release elasticated straps (one has been removed for clarity). This was standard practice with the Switlik Parachute Company whose trade name also appears on a patch next to the various stencils. The harness securing arrangement is also visible: an adjustable strap, stitched on the inner side of the bag and holding the handgrip, the ripcord and release cable

Right. The standard issue weapon is a .38 Smith & Wesson pistol carried in its regulation holster. The white cloth cartridge loops are a local improvisation. The weapon is secured by a 1917 Pattern lanyard still issued to USN personnel during World War 2. The weapon is displayed on an M-592 survival kit. The USN markings are clearly visible on the flying suit label and the inner pocket.

USAAF OFFICERS' SERVIC

Photographed in the United States during the summer of 1942, this officer wears the Blue Dress uniform adopted by American ground forces on 17 August 1938 (Army Regulation AR 600-38). This dark blue wool gabardine uniform comprises a roll collar dress coat and matching trousers. The four pockets have straight flaps sealed by service buttons. The four typical rank stripes appear on the cuffs in the form of gilt braid with a central piping in the service colour (dark blue here). Abandoned and reintroduced several times, the peculiar shoulder tabs were designed during the Civil War and are worn near the arm-holes. Piped with gilt bullion, the tabs feature the colour of the service and the rank insignia (the gilt oak leaves indicate the rank of major). The 'US' ciphers are worn on top of the lapels, above the Air Force's 'winged propeller' badge. Bars of service medals and qualification badges appear above the flap of the left pocket and include:
Pilot wings in gilt bullion on dark blue backing.
Distinguished Service Cross.
Silver Star.
Distinguished Flying Cross.
Air Medal with two oak leaves (indicating three awards).
Purple Heart.
World War 1 Victory Medal, (with one silver star device for a citation and three campaign bronze star devices).
Army of Occupation of Germany Medal.
American Defence Service Medal.
Chevalier de la Légion d'Honneur (France).
Croix de Guerre 1914-18 (France, with two palms indicating two mentions in army dispatches).
The two medals which have just been awarded and displayed on the officer's chest are the Legion of Merit (left) and the American Campaign Medal (right).

The cap has
blue crown
band indica
service arr
blue here).
was the
colour of
force as lo
answered t
command
grade office
peaks were a
by a double o
bullion, the o
large gilt e
screwed
front

The white cotton shirt is worn with a black silk tie. The dark blue gabardine trousers are piped in the service colour (piped breeches were issued to mounted troops) and worn with low black leather shoes.

By Pierre BESNARD

PRACTICALLY indistinguishable from their men in combat, American officers were nonetheless issued with a wide variety of service dresses well adapted to circumstances, climates and operational theatres.

Above left: Introduced on 11 May 1942, the Air Medal was awarded to armed forces personnel for distinguished conduct during a flight (after 8 September 1939).
Right: early, unofficial 15th Air Force bullion insignia (Italian-made).
From top to bottom:
J.R. Gaunt London-manufactured two-piece bombardier wings.
Navigator wings.
Aircrew Badge.
AMCRAFT-made pilot wings.
Below: Italian-made 15th Air Force bullion insignia.

RESS, 1942-1944

944: coming from North
this Major arrives at the
orce HQ in London.
w posting is reflected
insignia on his left
sleeve. He is clad in
ve Drab Service
m introduced in October
he tunic of which had been
ed modified in 1942
h the addition of a belt
of matching material which
ready apparent on Air
issue jackets. The
er tabs have gilt
metal oak leaves
ting rank while
rd ciphers and
ia appear on the
. The aircrew
and three bars of
e medals are
d above the left
t flap. Made of
ing material
dorned with the
can officer's
the cap has
a leather
rap
eak.

his arm, the
carries a
at,
ensible for
n Britain. The
authorised
ngs on this
ent introduced
43 are the rank
ia on the
ders. Because
ir colour, the
Drab, Light
e, gabardine
ers were
n as 'pinks'
re worn here
aced russet
er low laced
s.

During a furlough in Rome during 1944, it looks as if this Airforce officer finds it easier to navigate from the cockpit of his aircraft than on 'terra firma'. To make the most of his trip to the 'Eternal City', the airman has obtained a guide from the 'Special Services' Department. He is clad in the becoming Summer Dress introduced on 4 September 1944 and his cap is identical to the model shown at left but for the light khaki crown. In typical USAAF fashion, the crown stiffener has been removed. Of a similar cut to the olive drab models, the light khaki Tropical Worsted Tunic has no belt. Rank shoulder insignia appear in the shape of gilt metal oak leaves, while the 'US' monograms and branch insignia are pinned respectively to both sides of the collar and to the lapels. The embroidered gilt bullion pilot wings are pinned above the bar of service medals.

Above. The ribbons of the following service medals are worn above the left flap pocket: Distinguished Service Cross, Distinguished Flying Cross, Purple Heart and British Distinguished Flying Cross. As often with American officers, no campaign ribbons are displayed. The USAAF standard bullion sleeve insignia was made locally. The Overseas Service Stripes are mistakenly worn on the bottom on the left sleeve.

Below. An aerial chart of the North Atlantic provides the backdrop for this composition including from left to right and from top to bottom: 754th Bombardment Squadron (Heavy) leather patch (designed by Walt Disney Studios). Equipped with B-24s, this 8th Air Force unit took part in all major USAAF offensives over Northern Europe.
Bullion 8th Air Force insignia. Distinguished Flying Cross (created on 2 July 1926 as a reward for gallantry and distinguished service in the air). 8th US Air Force Weekly Air Intelligence Digest (for the week of 4-9 January 1943). British-made 9th Air Force embroidered insignia (displayed on a booklet recounting the exploits of the IXth Tactical Air Command, and published in Paris in 1945).
Variant of the 97th Fighter Squadron (15th Air Force) insignia (previously 12th Air Force). Equipped with P-38s, this unit participated in the North African and Italian campaigns.

The leather and canvas briefcase holds a few personal items, such as a dressing kit, while the bulk of the officer's belongings follows him about in a heavy trunk.

This airman displays some of the most significant details of his flying gear, including the lower part of the A-8B rubber oxygen mask with its tube and plug. The standard issue woollen scarf and the very popular sheepskin gauntlets complete the outfit which was designed to provide efficient protection from the cold. The jacket collar can be kept down by pressure studs or kept up around the neck with two leather straps and buckles. The sleeves have large leather patches to reduce wear. A large patch pocket with slanted opening can be seen on the right front at waist level.

The infla[...]
yellow B-3 r[...]
life jacket ope[...]
on CO2 an[...]
activated by a [...]
The B-3 was [...]
around the nec[...]
fastened by a [...]
belt connecte[...]
strap pa[...]
between the [...]

By Frédéric FINEL

1 **7 August 1943, Bury St Edmund Airforce Base in Britain. A bombardier is about to take his place in the glazed nose of a B-17F for a bombing·mission. Target: the Messerschmitt aircraft plant at Regensburg, deep in the heartland of Germany.**

Rayon (artificial silk) gloves were worn inside the leather gauntlets to protect the hands from frostbite.

The sheepskin A–6A leather boots have black rubber soles and front zip fasteners. The cuff strap is a 1944 modification (shown here, as no standard A-6 model was available when this 'Close-up' was put together).

Left. Top: 8th Air Force sleeve insignia introduced in 1943. Bottom: the bombardier wings officially described as 'a bomb dropping between wings superimposed over a circular target'. This badge was introduced on 10 July 1942.

BRITAIN, 1943

...AC (Quick ...able Chest) ...1 parachute has ...ack padding ...taining loops for ...aps. The reserve ... (held by the ... his left hand as ...ards the bomber) ...ept within reach ... missions and ...ed on for ...ency situations ...his 'chute was ...ed to the front of ...rness by two ...ooks.

...3 ...kin ...rs have ...atch ... s at ...vel. The ...egs are ...ith ... for ...access.

Close-up of the headgear. The B-6 sheepskin leather helmet is fitted with steel hooks suitable for the A-8, A-9 and A-8 oxygen masks. The sheepskin chinstrap is reinforced at the chin. The 'Skyway' goggles have a lacquered metal frame and grey rubber eyepieces.

Radio accessories include a T-30V throat microphone and a leather padded headset with wide grey rubber earpieces. The green A-8B rubber oxygen mask is fastened by removable leather straps.

USAAF paraphernalia displayed on an aerial chart of northern Europe: a small safety manual for emergency situations involving fire; bombardier wings, a transfer for leather garments, a standard USAAF embroidered badge, an A-11 wristwatch and a silk escape map.

The centrepiece of this display is undeniably the model bomb sporting the 392nd Bombardment Group insignia. It is seen next to a packet of Chesterfield cigarettes, matches and three wartime photographs showing a B-17E on the taxiway, a scene of 'fraternisation' between RAF and USAAF personnel and finally, the crew of a Flying Fortress returning from a mission. Above right: two 8th Air Force insignia. The bullion model at the top was locally manufactured.

AMERICAN P-47 D PILOT

Introduced in 1931, the A-2 flying jacket was made of horse hide leather and worn throughout the war - in spite of the Air Force Commander-in-Chief, General Arnold's, decision to have it replaced with a synthetic fur-lined cloth model in 1942. Progressive distribution of the new jacket began in 1944 resulting in the A-2 being worn until the end of the conflict as both a flying and walking-out garment.

The S-1 parachute harness typical socket attachments seat parachute was introd in 1942 and rema practically uncha throughout the war. A Aid Packet is fasten the harr The rubberized cotto

'Mae Wes preser compose two envelc

containin infla rubber fed CO_2 be

Halesworth Air Base, Suffolk,1943, at 9.15am on a chilly November morning. A P-47 D pilot of 56th Fighter Group is about to board his aircraft for a long mission: escorting B-17s on a bombing raid over Germany.

As often with US 8th and 9th Air Force pilots, the man is kitted out in a mixture of British and American equipment. ❑

Compatible with all types of harness, the AN-6510 seat parachute was used throughout the conflict. Six elastic strips pull the parachute bag apart when the black sheathed ripcord (on the left) is tugged. The 8th Air Force shoulder insignia is painted on the left sleeve of the flying jacket which displays the rank insignia on its shoulder tabs. The RAF sheepskin flying boots have laced lowers, zipped uppers and cuff tightening straps.

A holster for a .45 1911 A1 Colt pistol, two spare magazines and a field dressing in its standard M–1942 pocket are suspended from the 1936 Pattern pistol belt (hidden here by the jacket's waistband).

The so-c 'pink' offi trousers were intended service d garment but la worn by p alongside the k serge mo

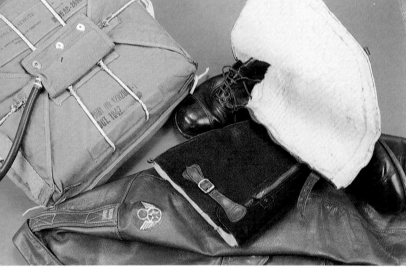

BRITAIN, 1943

...ened by an inner ...onal zipper, the ...icated cuffed 1941 ...rn gauntlets are also ...owed from the RAF. ...ring the forearm, ...e gauntlets were ...in preference to ...merican ...els as they ...ded better ...ction ...st fire.

Worn with American B-7 goggles, the Type C Pattern 42 leather helmet is also of British origin. The sunglasses are Bausch & Lomb. The 'A-10 Revised' oxygen mask is fitted with a microphone lead manufactured in Britain on behalf of the AAF (Army Air Forces).

For high altitude flights needing an oxygen mask, sunglasses were preferred to the B-7 goggles which restricted the field of vision. The goggles, however, came in handy in case of windscreen damage or when the pilot had to bail out.

By Jacques Alluchon

Front view of the harness showing the reinforcements, the typical socket fittings as well as the kapok-filled cushion used for comfort. The sheathed ripcord is also visible.

...S-1 ...ess is ...with ...-2 ...ival kit ...nally ...gned for jungle ...ival ...oment and ...here as a ...ion for ...oved comfort ...e cramped ...ines of the ...s' cockpit.

The RAF issue Pattern 1943 sheepskin boots are made of two components: laced lowers with toe cap and uppers tightened by a zipper and buckled strap. If forced down over enemy territory, the airmen could cut off the uppers to make the boots look like ordinary shoes, hence their nickname of 'escape boots'. This comfortable footwear had no equivalent in the US Army Air Forces inventory.

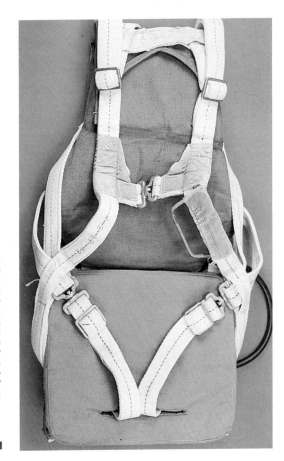

AMERICAN P-47 D, PILOT — BRITAIN, 1943

Displayed on a British aerial chart: a B-3 life preserver, RAF Pattern 1941 gauntlets (one is unzipped so as to show its markings), B-7 goggles with their case and an A-10 Revised oxygen mask (displayed next to the leather helmet). The Bausch & Lomb glasses are shown alongside their leather covered case.

Several objects taken by the pilot for his long flight are shown on a British silk escape map (carried in the 'Maps Only' folder at the bottom). Left: the 'First Aid Kit, Parachute' with its complete contents. Originally intended for American aircrew, this kit was later issued to paratroopers and includes: a field dressing, a tourniquet and a small syringe of morphine (displayed on its cardboard container). Right: an emergency Bail Out Ration. The D–Ration and the two Hershey chocolate bars were flight provisions. To the left of the chocolate: a standard pocket compass and, above, the A-11 Bulova issue watch and a packet of cigarettes to ease tension during long flights (whenever the oxygen mask wasn't worn, that is!)

Left.
The '50 missions' crush cap. The sunglasses shown here were a favourite among American airmen. The control dates are stencilled in black on the front of the B-4 life preserver.

A-2 horse hide leather flying jacket

Field dressing (on issue to airborne forces).

M-1936 belt and M-1910 ammunition pouches.

Aeronautical chart of Normandy.

A-10 line glove

Leather service shoes.

By Frédéric FINEL

A 1st Lieutenant is about to climb into his P-51 Mustang. His next mission: supporting Allied ground forces clawing their way off the Normandy beaches.

Pilot wings.

Left.
On his return, the pilot describes his mission. During the flight, he was pitted against some of the few remaining Luftwaffe fighters which once ruled the skies of western Europe. Thanks to his peculiar stance, the harness of the cushioned seat parachute is shown to advantage. The non-regulation Colt holster suspended from the belt is a modified M-5 shoulder model.

IGHTER PILOT, 1944

Right.
Headgear. The AN-6530 goggles are held by elasticated straps. The A-14 rubber oxygen mask is fastened to the helmet by pressure studs. Radio accessories include a mask microphone and R-14 earphones. The insignia on the wool shirt include the 1st Lieutenant silver bars and the air force winged propeller, worn respectively on the left and right lapels.

AN-1936 seat parachute.

On standard issue to American forces, the sturdy and comfortable woollen trousers were well suited to combat missions.

Right.
The manufacturer's label is sewn inside the chamois-lined headgear. The USAAF property stamp appears above the headset earpiece. The leather jacket label and the patch pockets with pressure studs are noteworthy. The reverse side of the pilot wings with its typical fastening pin. A-10 gloves with knitted cuffs and lining. The manufacturer's label is sewn inside the chamois-lined headgear. The USAAF property stamp appears above the headset earpiece. The leather jacket label and the patch pockets with pressure studs are noteworthy. The reverse side of the pilot wings with its typical fastening pin. A-10 gloves with knitted cuffs and lining.

ACKNOWLEDGEMENTS

The authors wishe to thank all the specialists, militaria dealers and collectors who kindly supplied photographs to illustrate this book.

PHOTO CREDITS

Lech ALEXANDROWICZ
Philippe CHARBONNIER
Jon GAWNE
François VAUVILLIER

Design: Philippe CHARBONNIER, Jean-Marie MONGIN, Patrick LESIEUR. © PLST
UK Co-ordinator: Alexandra GARDINER

ISBN : 2 908 182 27 0
Publisher' s number : 2-908182.
Published by **Histoire & Collections**
19, avenue de la République.
75011 Paris, France.
Tél. : International *(1) 40.21.18.20*
Fax : International *(1) 40.21.97.55*

Editorial composition : *Macintosh II FX, Quadra 650, X Press* and Adobe *Illustrator*
Photography *: SCIPE*, Paris.
Colour separation *: Point 11, Ogerault,* Paris.

Printed by *SIB*, Saint-Léonard, France, on 28 February 1994

ISBN: *2 908 182 27 0*
HISTOIRE ET COLLECTIONS, P.O. Box 327, Poole, Dorset BH 15 2RG UK